ON HORSEBACK

BY THE SAME AUTHOR

Rogue Lion Safaris
Hong Kong Belongers
Miss Chance

Simon Barnes

ON HORSEBACK

SELECTED JOURNALISM

HarperCollins*Publishers*

HarperCollins*Publishers*
77–85 Fulham Palace Road,
Hammersmith, London W6 8JB

www.**fire**and**water**.com

Published by HarperCollins*Publishers* 2000
1 3 5 7 9 8 6 4 2

A catalogue record for this book
is available from the British Library

ISBN 0 00 257215 X

Typeset in Bembo by Palimpsest Book Production Limited,
Polmont, Stirlingshire

Printed and bound in Great Britain by
Clays Ltd, St Ives plc

Contents

	Foreword	vii
	Introduction	xi
1	Horse-whispering (part one)	1
2	A morning with Venetia	6
3	Mark Phillips, my teacher	11
4	The voice: Sir Peter O'Sullevan	16
5	A leg-up on Desert Orchid	21
6	Circle of folly	26
7	Learning to be Lester	31
8	On the cutting edge with Martin Pipe	36
9	A brief guide to breeding a champion	41
10	Stable lads: a race of heroes	51
11	Mark Todd: the best ever	59
12	Why fillies are politically incorrect	64
13	No one likes us, we don't care	69
14	Sheikh Mo (part one)	74
15	A gallop with a racing dynasty	82
16	The ride of a lifetime	87
17	A spot of mindless violence	92

18	Riding side-saddle	95
19	A day at Pony Club camp	100
20	Peta Beckett (part one)	103
21	The pig-cart horse	110
22	Supervising my string on Newmarket Heath	115
23	Carl Hester: a brush with perfection	120
24	Dressage for the blind	125
25	Betting: Barney Curley (and me)	130
26	The greatest show-jumper ever	138
27	One Man: the reasons why	143
28	Sheikh Mo (part two)	148
29	A triumph	153
30	A victory	158
31	Horse-whispering (part two)	163
32	'Four-in-hand' Barnes	172
33	There but for the grace of God . . .	177
34	An afternoon as a champion	185
35	Just like Clint	190
36	Wisdom and folly	195
37	How to be a prodigy	200
38	On Watership Down	205
39	Riding the dressage camels	210
40	Starting afresh	215

Foreword

To tell the truth, I always resisted the idea of writing about horses. I thought it would be just a bit too much. Horses are so much a part of my daily life, and I have so much of an emotional stake in horses, that I thought that anything I wrote about them would be best delivered in a plain brown wrapper.

But then everything came up horsey: *The Times* asked me to write Talking Horse, a weekly column about horses, and various horsey magazines asked me to do some stuff for them. And I found myself loving it.

Every piece you write in such circumstances is for a deadline: and for a certain edition of a publication with a limited shelf life. But when you write anything, particularly something that means a good deal to you, you try to be consistent, and you hope that your work actually adds up to something. I hope that what I have written about horses provides a consistent view of horses and horse people: and of the contract that exists between them.

The pieces are presented pretty well as they appeared: I have made a few small changes here and there, occasionally to correct an error that had crept in during production, sometimes to cut out a line that is repeated elsewhere in the book. I'm afraid journos do tend to repeat themselves: it is this – rather than making things up – that is the real vice of the profession. I hope I have told each joke no more than half a dozen times, anyway . . .

The backbone of the book is pieces from *The Times*, presented, mostly, in chronological order: I thought it would be more fun to have the pieces come at you more or less at random, rather than bunched together in some arbitrary way. Besides, if I stuck all the dressage pieces together, it would put too many people off. I have taken some pieces from *The Spectator*, and put them in out of chronological order, using them to offer a comment on other, longer pieces.

I would like to offer thanks first to every person who has given me time and the freedom of the stable yard and, often, a horse to ride. I have had some memorable experiences with some memorable horses: I hope I have done them all justice.

I also owe thanks to Keith Blackmore and David Chappell at *The Times*, who got me to write about horses, and to George Brock for permission to reprint the pieces here. Thanks also to Boris Johnson at *The Spectator*, who generously allowed me to reprint some pieces from my weekly column. Thanks to Richard Vadon at the BBC, who produced a series of talks I gave for Radio 4, which included the pieces used as introduction. Thanks also to Alison Bridge at *Horse & Rider*, for whom I now write a regular column.

Best thanks to all horsey people who have given me encouragement, and who have written to me saying that this or that piece got it right. These things matter more than the writer of the letters can ever guess. Thanks also to that person all journalists need: the good sub.

Finally, of course, thanks to the horses themselves: all the lovely chance rides I have had. But most particular thanks to my own: Dolly Dolores, in foal as I write, and her strapping son, Bullseye.

Final thought before we begin: the best wind in the world is the one that blows between a horse's ears (Arab proverb).

Introduction

For my introduction, I present a transcript of a talk I gave on Radio 4, in a series called *Sporting Sermons*.

Britain is a nation of horse-lovers. It's riders they can't stand. Most people are keen to talk about their obsessions: one of the first skills any horsey person learns is how to turn conversation away from horses.

I know why you like horses, whips, spurs, boots, nudge nudge. As if it were the most tremendous joke and they were the only person ever to think of it.

My own patent conversation stopper, when asked 'Why do you like horses?' is to reply: 'Because I haven't discovered boys yet.' A friend of mine, female, has invented an even more effective method, one guaranteed to kill a conversation stone dead. 'You should see the size of my horse's willy,' she says. Oddly enough, no one ever mentions the subject – horses, that is – again.

I remember keeping an appointment at the King's Head in Islington, a not untrendy establishment, having got delayed and so gone from horse to train to town without stopping to change.

Piece of advice to all horse people – do not wear jods and riding boots at the King's Head in Islington.

I was treated like a slum landlord with an I-love-Hitler tattoo, upper-class twit of the year, a torturer of innocent animals, an enemy to all progressive thought, a sexual deviant, a political oppressive, a social inadequate. And so rich it was obscene.

The last part is not, alas, true. I have frequently taken taxis to or from horsey places, and I always get the same question. 'Blimey. Expensive hobby, isn't it?'

Hobby? Do you call breathing oxygen a hobby?

And as for expensive, well, it all depends on your priorities. I used to travel to and from shows with a group of raucous cockney ladies. You could hear us lot coming a mile off: it was like a wagonful of magpies.

One was a secretary, one bred monkeys for a living, another worked at the checkout at Sainsbury's. They drove old bangers, the lorry was held together with baling twine, they dressed – well, warmly. The horses gleamed. And they could ride, too: we picked up a fair few ribbons between us.

That, by the way, is horsey jargon for doing pretty well, and so winning a rosette. I'll try and keep the jargon to a minimum, but it does tend to break out every now and then. That is part of the joy of it all.

And so to national hate objects. At one stage, Princess Anne was the most unpopular Royal since Nero. Her crime, of course, was riding horses: and doing so extremely well. She was European three-day event champion, which takes a bit of doing.

Every eventer takes a tumble now and then: it became a national obsession trying to get a picture of Princess Anne falling off her horse, preferably into the water. The sight of Princess Anne on a horse brought out the latent Bastille-stormer that lurks inside every royalist Brit: the sight of her tumbling into the water was as good as a guillotining.

As for Mark Phillips, the person she married at the height of her horsey period: he was regarded as a national joke, the thickest bloke in the history of horsey Britain. I once spent a couple of days as his pupil, and he is a brilliant teacher. But it is horses he is brilliant at – and that is considered very much the same thing as being stupid. Horse people must either ignore the outside world or get used to a good deal of hostility.

And if you want to experience absolutely lethal hatred, try riding a horse on the road. Mere road rage becomes murderous and maniacal fury when a horse is involved. I've been hit twice, or at least, my horse has, both times from almost insane – you'd have thought literally certifiable – impatience. Riding flat-out round a cross-country course is merely terrifying: riding along a busy road is as profound an experience of fear and loathing as a normal person can easily get.

I've had it all: people leaning out of cars to swear at me; people sneaking up behind and roaring the engine or sounding the horn; people passing at 50 miles an hour with an inch to spare. Oh, certainly, most drivers are kind and generous and all riders do an awful lot of waving and smiling. And we can all, every single one of us, recount a list as long as a lunge-line of near-death experiences.

Oh, they hate riders all right, the Brits do – but, oh, how they love their horses. Has there ever been a horse as greatly loved as Desert Orchid? Big, beautiful and above all grey: you could tell him a mile off. Brits love their horses to be grey: that is to say, recognisable. In fact, the greatest skill of the racehorse trainer is to be able to tell the owner, without giving offence, which horse is his.

But everyone can tell the only grey in the race, and Dessie had a million owners. And not only was he big and beautiful and grey, he was fallible: beautifully and endearingly fallible. He hated running left-handed at Cheltenham: he only won the big race of the season, the Cheltenham Gold Cup, but once.

A gorgeous horse all right, a creature of strutting, posing dominance, like a grown-up version of Chris Eubank. Dessie is the sort that would make anybody who sat on his back feel just a little bit like God almighty and I know. I have sat on him. I have sat on him, patting that hard white neck, while the horse held himself as if he measured a good 25 hands, gazing loftily and serenely at the clouded hills, and printing his proud hooves in the receiving earth.

I spend a lot of time with horses and with horse people, not only in my private life, with my own two wonderful and dodgy animals, but in my professional life. Of recent years, I seem to spend less and less of my life trying to be a renaissance man, and more and more of it as a horse writer, like the Honourable Schoolboy in the Le Carré novel.

In most of my journalistic life, I have rather specialised in getting thrown out of places despite holding all the right credentials. But I can walk as I please in just about every stable in the land: racing, dressage, eventing, endurance riding – anywhere where there are horses and horse people. Because I know the password, you see.

I can do the funny handshake, I speak the lingo, I can pat horses, and my body language screams the message: I am happy here. I am at ease. And without claiming to be the world's number one horse whisperer, I know that the horses know this too.

Horses read body language just as much as the horse people; or to be accurate, much better. With horses, body language is the primary rather than a secondary means of communication:

naturally they are better at reading it than us. Horses read humans better than humans read horses: not a shadow of a doubt.

All of which gives me the chance to meet horses and horse people, of every kind, of every discipline. One of the odd things about the horsey life is how compartmentalised it is: how dressage people hate show-jumpers and show-jumpers despise dressage, and everybody not in racing hates everybody in racing.

These barriers are beginning to disappear, with the benefits of cross-training becoming apparent in the forward-thinking people in every discipline. Cross-training has become the nouvelle cuisine of horsey life. But traditionally, it has generally been the case that no one hates horsey people as much as horsey people themselves.

But me, I go from yard to yard, dropping names, listening to Michael Stoute's bajan twang in his Newmarket racing yard, listening to Carl Hester's chorus-boy drawl at his centre of dressage excellence – and all I see is the stuff we all have in common. Which is a kind of madness, a kind of infection of the blood.

Sheikh Mohammed al Maktoum, defence minister of Dubai, is the world's richest racehorse owner. And standing beside him – sweet name-drop, that one – on the Albahatri gallop in Newmarket, I am struck not by the light-years' distance apart in wealth, but by what we have in common.

We both have too many horses – I have two – and we both spend too much money on them, and we both occasionally complain about it, and neither of us would think of existing for a second without them.

The love is the same, or if you prefer, the dementia. To be with a horse and, also, to seek to improve the horse. To fulfil the potential of the horse. Put like this, it almost sounds sensible. But no: it is a disorder of the blood.

Sometimes it seems that this disorder is inherited, a genetic aberration. I always thought I disproved this: brought up in Streatham, never having much to do with horses. Horses, like religion and measles, are more easily dealt with in childhood. Horsiness struck me with mad born-again convert fervour when I was nearly 30. I broke out in a raging temperature and kept the fire stoked to this day.

But then the same thing happened to my sister, and to all my nieces. We were all brought up most carefully as townees: whence this disorder of the blood?

And I remembered that my grandfather had been horsey. He became townee and respectable and middle-class and aspirational and even moved to Birmingham to do so, but before this happened he was a country and a horsey boy and served four years in Salonika in the First World War as a sergeant in the horse artillery.

Blood will out. It has just skipped a generation. Now my father has to come to terms with the fact that there are no fewer than seven horses in his family.

We are banned from using the H-word at the lunch table, but we mutter between courses about hackamores and fetlocks and stifles and kimblewicks, and I'll tell you what I'd do if it was my horse, and it is all glorious. And the rest of the family hates it.

But why horses? Now I have a passion for wilderness. My favourite place on earth is the Luangwa valley in Zambia. And every time I leave, my kind friends of the Valley ask if I will miss it, back in the civilised British countryside. How can I bear to be away from wilderness?

But I never am. You can take a horse out of the wilderness, but you can never take the wilderness out of a horse. A dog offers uncritical love, and is wholly a creature of the hearth and the human: he has forgotten that he was once a wolf.

But a horse has never ceased to be a wild wary animal of the plains. Watch that row of heads hanging over the half-doors of a stable block just before evening feed, hear the soft whickering chuckle they give as they hear the clatter of the feed-buckets. It is this that gets you: that eternal paradox of cosy domesticity and untamed wildness.

There is something in a horse's mind, a horse's heart that you can never quite reach, never quite know. And also, there is something in his heart and mind that you can know very well indeed. That is the heart of the paradox.

But a horse always contains that quantum of wilderness. And you don't tame it, no. You don't try. Wildness is the key to it all: to extravagant jumping, to the powerful gymnastic of dressage, to the victory on the racetrack. You seek not dominance but a partnership: you seek not to dam the wildness but to canalise it.

The best of all horses balance on a razor's edge of control. I have ridden a Grand Prix dressage horse in piaffe and found staggering power, balance, obedience. And then I made an error: and the horse leapt and reared like a skyrocket. Born to be wild, born to be tame. The paradox of nature and nurture walks with a horse and his rider at every stride.

And now on to the most scary part of all. I must tell you about the time I penetrated the most hated organisation in the country: the time I went to Pony Club camp.

My first feeling was the most terrible regret that I had not been to Pony Club camp when I was a boy. With a ration of ten girls to every chap, the most scrofulous wizened shrimp of a lad is a strutting sex god.

But on to the junior camp, and the ten-year-olds at the bareback jumping class, and within two minutes I found myself not observing but catching ponies and legging brave lower-lip-biting girls back onto their animals again.

People think that every Pony Club child is by definition spoiled: well, my observation is that parents are perfectly capable of spoiling children without the help of a pony.

And, in fact, a pony is likely to keep a child in order: ponies don't, on the whole, take to being treated as playthings. Half the ponies I saw were on their fourth or fifth child: decent little beasts, handed from family to family through the country grapevine, parents not bursting with lolly but ready to give horses the priority.

It's about learning. Learning about horses, sure. Also learning about learning: the number of dyslexic and dyspraxic children who come to an accommodation with life through horses is quite astounding.

But there is a deeper and far more terrible lesson to be learned in the Pony Club and in anything to do with horses. It is learning about love. A child learns that love involves all kinds of terrible responsibilities, generally ones that need to be met when you least feel like doing so – in the pouring rain at the wrong end of the day and you exhausted and late for something else and your fingers dropping from your hands with cold.

And you learn that love is not a straightforward matter. Horses will ignore a bully and trample on a doormat: shut their ears to shouting, close their minds to a fool. It is an inexorable rule of life: you always end up standing before your horse exactly as you are. And you learn that love is the most difficult and dangerous subject in the world.

And so a final piece of advice to people who think of involving themselves in horses. Don't. Horses break the bank, they break your bones, they break your heart. And I plan to give them up myself. Sure. I'll give them up on the same day that I give up oxygen.

1

Horse-whispering (Part One)

Most of these pieces are written on the basis that there is something magical about horses: something other-worldly. But there is a deep desire in us to find something magical in horsey *people*: the book and film *The Horse Whisperer* is all about this hunger for a miracle-worker. We want to believe in a miraculous form of communication between our two species: and that some people have this gift of communication to a miraculous degree.

I had naturally seen Monty Roberts on television, and been massively intrigued by his technique of interspecific communication, called join-up. Also, I knew an utterly sceptical friend who had, in desperation, called in Richard Maxwell, a Monty disciple, to help her out. And it worked: the horse is now

> threatening to become a Grand Prix dressage horse; there is no higher category.
>
> So very early on in the life of Talking Horse, I got in touch with Maxwell. And, not being short of cheek, I asked if I could go into the round pen and do it myself.

I have spent about 20 years trying to force the door open, and I think I've done quite well. I have pushed and shoved and hammered, and I have managed to open up a fair chink. And if I look through it, I can get a good idea of the beauties that lie on the far side. Twenty years of shoving. Now they tell me. Now they tell me that the door opens inwards.

I write these words in a fair amount of emotional turmoil. Because I have visited a man whose work redefines the relationship between human beings and horses – and that is what all the horse sports are about, from racing through dressage to Pony Club games.

In Richard Maxwell's yard, not far from Newmarket, is a racehorse that won't race. It is like the famous Hamlet cigar ad; he simply refuses to leave the starting stalls. There is a dressage horse covered in scars; it is given to violet self-mutilation. There is an eventing horse that rears up and bends backwards like a banana. It sometimes does this on one leg. There is also a child's pony that refuses to get on its trailer. 'No snobbery here,' Maxwell said.

And there are half a dozen young horses that must be backed. This is horse jargon, not for placing a bet, but for teaching a horse to accept a rider. The traditional term for the initial training of a young horse is 'breaking'. Maxwell talks about 'starting' and in that semantic nicety lies a revolution: something that calls into question the countless millennia of the relationship between man and horse. One other thing about the yard: there is not a single whip.

Maxwell is – already I can see him wince – a horse whisperer.

Naturally he feels somewhat ambivalent about the blockbusting book that brought the new school of horsemanship into the popular mind.

Maxwell is glad that people have heard of it all – not least because it brings him clients, young horses for starting, gone-wrong horses for curing. But he is not a phoney miracle-worker, he is not a faith healer. Just another practical horseman.

Yet he has worked what looked like miracles with rogue racehorses, horses that had been written off. Some would not enter the stalls, other were simply too aggressive. 'Taking Vettori into the stalls was like being trapped in a broom cupboard with Mike Tyson,' Maxwell said. Vettori went on to win a classic, the French 2,000 Guineas. Stelvio, another write-off, won the Queen's Vase at Royal Ascot; La Confederation, once told never to darken a racecourse again, picked up a group two race.

It was the Queen who got Maxwell started. She may have said that the modern world is leaving her behind but she delighted in the sound of revolution when she heard of Monty Roberts. Roberts is the man behind the new school. He calls it, prosaically enough, 'join-up'.

Join-up is utterly convincing to almost anybody who witnesses it. Maxwell thought it was rubbish. He was training to be an instructor in the Household Cavalry at the time and was recommended – polite word in the better regiments for 'ordered' – to watch a Monty Roberts demonstration. 'We sat there like schoolkids and picked holes in it,' Maxwell said.

But Maxwell subsequently found himself with 35 horses to 'back' in two weeks. This, by the way, is impossible. Maxwell and a colleague did it by using join-up. Not a single injury was sustained by any of the horses or horsemen.

Maxwell went on to work for Roberts and subsequently left the Household Cavalry and went to California to work for Roberts on his home ground. Then he set up on his own in England. And, naturally, he has had a good share of being despised and rejected. The military tradition penetrates all aspects of horsiness: there is a right and a wrong way to do things, and you do not question it. Racing, in particular, is not so much indifferent as hostile. In truth, most people in racing are too much involved with today and tomorrow; there is never any time for a radical rethink of the fundamental tenets of horsemanship. Doubts only come when a horse goes thoroughly wrong. For many, Maxwell is merely a last resort, the man to go to when all else fails. Naturally, he would prefer his method to be a first resort.

Back to the yard where Maxwell is working a young mare for the first time. A tough individual: the sort, in animal behaviour jargon, who would become an alpha female, the dominant mare in her herd. Maxwell was seeking, by eye contact and body language, to establish himself as the dominant animal of the two.

'She doesn't want to accept me,' he said, without for a second taking his eyes from the mare. 'She has a lifetime of baggage to get rid of.' And as I watched, the daily miracle occurred: the mare accepted the dominant animal; horse and human 'joined up'.

Bring on a new horse, and a new human. The horse was not a problem animal but an ordinary decent sort, belonging to Maxwell, called Murphy. It was a human that was the problem. I know. I was that human.

But in less than a minute, I had Murphy cantering away from me, at my decision. Within a couple of minutes, I could change his direction at will. Looking hard at his inside eye as he circled around me, my body turned towards him. This was, I learnt, a form of considerable aggression. I was sending the horse away, as if in punishment for some misdeed.

Roberts learnt this from watching feral horses in the United

States. They send away a horse that has stepped out of line, upset a dominant animal. He is barred from the herd. He may affect unconcern, but more than anything else in life, he wants to be back. It is his nature. Also, solitude can be fatal – a lone horse is ten times more vulnerable to predators. He needs, above all things, to be part of the herd.

Murphy cocked his right ear towards me. It was the beginning of a request to return to the herd. I made a concession: I permitted him to trot, moderating my body language in imitation of Maxwell. The horse lowered his head, chewed with his lips, poked out his tongue. It was a plaintive request for forgiveness. I forgave. I turned away from him, my eye leaving his. I stopped moving.

After about 30 seconds, I felt a soft nudge on my shoulder. The horse had 'joined up' with me. And so, for about 15 minutes, I walked about. Very quickly, then slowly, sometimes stopping dead. Everything I did, Murphy did a pace behind me.

It was stunning, and I was stunned. It is not something the horse learns. Horses have always known it. It is humans that have had to learn it; and then to show the horse that they have done so. In this way, humans have penetrated deeper than ever before into the border country that lies between our two species.

Perhaps I have made all this sound a bit touchy-feely happy-clappy. It is not. It is very tough indeed: to send a horse away is a severe scolding, in some ways more severe than a whipping. But it is how horses deal with horses. And with this method, the way is open for a deeper understanding – a deeper mutual understanding – than ever before. I'm a better horseman than I was last week.

The Times
11 October 1997

2

A Morning with Venetia

It is possible that the perceptive reader may discern in the author a pronounced weakness for horsey ladies. Venetia Williams is the first of many such ladies to be found in this collection.

I have always felt at home in all stable yards, infinitely preferring a visit to yard or gallops to a visit to the races. I like to meet both horses and horse people on their own ground: where they are truly themselves. All yards have different vibes, invariably reflecting the nature of the trainer.

National Hunt always prides itself on being the most down-to-earth of all the horsey sports. But it is only at a yard like this one that the horses are not so much down-to-earth as covered in earth from head to toe. This was not the only reason why this yard became one of my favourites to visit.

Can I tell you what it felt like, to see a row of filthy horses poking their heads over the half-doors of their boxes? It felt like home, that's what it felt like. Back at the yard where my own beasts live, and me wondering precisely how much grooming I was going to bother with before I tacked up and got on with it.

Turn-out, horse people call it. People like myself, who keep horses simply because they like being with horses, always like to turn them out into a field for a good slice of their day. The horse is happier turned out than he is standing in his box all day, and there's an end to the matter.

Racing yards are very different. They are result-oriented; there is no other option. If you are any good in racing, you start out with high hopes, and very quickly come to have high expectations. And part of that involves keeping your horses fit and sound. What? Turn them out so they can run about crazily, and kick each other, and roll? It is not a risk worth considering.

But there was a chunky chestnut in the middle of his mad ten minutes, charging from one end of his paddock to the other, New Zealand rug aflap, as merry a horse as you could wish to see. And there in the boxes were all the muddy faces. And there were the horses being tacked up for second lot. Mud on their faces, and matted into their manes in natty dreadlocks. Well, obviously this was some half-cocked, amateurish outfit, some ramshackle backwoodsman involved in racing for a bit of fun. One of jump racing's archetypes, a 'character' who even has the odd winner now and then. Except it wasn't: it was the most successful yard in the country.

In percentage terms, anyway. Last season, Venetia Williams's strike-rate – percentage of winners to runners – was 28.7 per cent, with 33 winners from 115 runners. That beat Martin Pipe, David Nicholson, everybody.

So it made sense to pay a visit to a new force in the sport. She has Celtic Abbey running at Cheltenham today and I expected to find a yard electric with anticipation.

I found nothing of the kind. The soothing quality of a racing yard? May as well talk about the predictability of horse racing, the cowardice of jump jockeys, the poverty of bookmakers. But all the same, that was what I found: a racing yard, an oasis of calm.

'Good at it? I don't know that I am good at it.' And Williams laughed, as if amused at the very idea. 'Perhaps last season was a flash in the pan.' Calm trainers are in the same category as Muhammadan Popes, but there I was, exchanging easy jokes with a trainer who exuded a positive aura of calm.

The dirty horse is not a whim or a gimmick. It represents a philosophy: that a horse is happiest when allowed to be a horse. And therefore, the theory continues, more likely to stay sane and sound and healthy, and therefore more likely to win races.

Williams's horses graze, with their heads down, they move about, they socialise. In a small way, they have control over their lives: a limited autonomy.

Horsey people will often say they turn a horse out 'so he knows he's a horse'. Williams, maximising not much acreage, has divided two large fields into small paddocks, in which selected pairs of horses can scoff and frolic. The physiological arguments for this are convincing; the psychological ones irresistible, and last season's results say anything more that needs to be said.

At least, they do until the new season starts in earnest. American sports people talk about 'the sophomore jinx', the failure of the promising rookie to train on. This is not quite Williams's second season; but it is the second season in which people are noticing her. Flash in the pan? We'll see.

She apologises, with only mild insincerity, for being unable to tell me that she had always been consumed by an ambition to be a top trainer. No, she had a much more modest target most of her adult life: to be the top amateur rider, until she broke her neck in a fall at Worcester.

She was paralysed from the neck down. Only for a matter of minutes: but a few minutes like that stay with you for ever. She left hospital two months later with a new focus.

It was a focus sharpened rather gradually. She worked with Pipe and Michael Dickinson, two almost disturbingly goal-driven men, before setting up on her own.

The horses before us were working on their interval training: an easy, lobbing hand-canter up five furlongs; the same back down again. Easy chat with a group of owners, a lovely morning in the Wye Valley. Kicking on into a big stretchy canter up the sharp incline. Lobbing back. Relaxed, contented horses, glowing and snorting in the autumn sun. Best time of year for anyone in jumping.

It is a nice operation, this: and there is almost no clue at all of the sleepy power behind it all, though there was just a bit of a hint when Williams gave me a lift to Worcester races. The sporty BMW is driven with more flair than patience; more decision than apology.

She is like no racing trainer I have met. There was so little sense of power or triumph, or of weight of responsibility. Rather, you felt, a trace of self-doubt: and the constant mastery of it. In fact, I did not feel as if I had been to a racing yard at all.

I was reminded more of the great female eventers, people like Lucinda Green and Mary King. There was the same ease of manner, the same easy self-deprecation. The same feeling for horses as sentient creatures, as individuals.

Williams has gone beyond the early delights, when each winner is a heady and impossible triumph. The pressures of starting up are considerable, but the real pressure starts when winners are not hopes but serious expectations. 'Instead of being wonderfully exciting, a winner is now . . . something of a relief, more than anything else.' And the inevitable self-deprecating tag: 'Rather stupid, really.'

Self-doubt, self-deprecation: these are not, in the main, the way goal-oriented males present themselves. Williams is not putting up a front intended to deceive. The truth of the matter is that self-doubt is a way in which some people are strong-minded. In their constant questioning of themselves and what they do, they are seeking real answers. More: they are seeking real perfection.

Perfection in racing is impossible. Perhaps the closest anyone gets to 100 per cent perfection is around the 28.7 mark. And like the Red Queen, Williams knows that it takes all the running you can do to stay in the same place. Advancing takes something more.

Williams has something more, I suspect. If I had horses in training, I know which yard I'd send them to, if she'd have them. Regardless of whether my priority was happy horses or winners.

The Times

15 November 1997

3

Mark Phillips, My Teacher

One of the great things about being a horsey person is that you always have something to say to another horsey person. Meeting someone with the complicated past of Mark Phillips is fraught with problems, the more especially as he is very self-protective.

But I was invited to attend a riding clinic in Ireland, at Ashford Castle, one of those privileges that occasionally fall in a journalist's way. It was all frightfully up-market: I confess I rather acquired a taste for leaving my riding boots outside the door, and finding them gleaming the following morning.

But the nub of the business was Phillips. There is a powerful didactic streak in many, many top horse people: they not only do it themselves, but they want to pass it on. I was lucky to be his pupil for a couple of days.

The thing about meeting Mark Phillips is that it brings you straight into a don't-mention-the-war situation. I know I'm not going to mention That Family, but how can I make him know I know?

It is a delicate piece of social manoeuvring and the etiquette books don't help you a bit. Which means that there is always a wariness about Phillips. It is something that everybody who meets him must deal with and naturally, and rightly, that counts double for a journalist.

I have known many a horse with the same kind of air about him: big, strapping fellows of imposing presence and massive self-confidence, but who are always likely to spook at anything they take a dislike to. Phillips is filled with conversational spookiness: no doubt a defensive reaction that comes not from his nature, but from hard-won experience.

Who could blame him? There came a period in two or three horse-filled days with Phillips, when the horse I had been loaned, a dominant type who insisted on being at the front, had to walk alongside the lead horse, which was ridden, of course, by Phillips. Horsey etiquette demands a little, but not too much, chat at such a point. So I made an amiable remark about the pleasures of a young family – and at once prompted that infinitesimal spook, that sampling of every remark for intrusiveness or impertinence.

I followed with a joke about my own domestic life – this is just small talk, Mark, honest – and the tiny point of tension was resolved and he made a joke of his own. Just two chaps on horses, talking about things such as life and horses. Life should be like that.

Phillips has a strange facial tic. It may be physiologically based for all I know, but it is utterly characteristic of the man, nonetheless. His eyes half close and stay that way – half-blinked, ungiving, self-protecting. It is a slightly disturbing expression. You suspect that he has grown to require more personal space than most.

The trouble is that Phillips has suffered the tragedy of being famous for the wrong reason. He played a long season or two before he was written out of that long-running soap, The Windsors, and the thing about that kind of fame is that it leaves you typecast.

Phillips is seen now as the upper-class twit who doesn't know about anything except (maybe) horses. So the questions I was asked repeatedly as I returned from Ireland and three days in his company were: how much of an idiot is he?; does he really know anything about horses?

Well, I reply, he's only about the best in the world. There or thereabouts, anyway. Which made the idea of spending time under his personal instruction intriguing, to say the least.

So, when I got on the borrowed horse, it was not auspicious when the animal's first move was to charge off sideways with his nose a good deal higher than his ears. Well, I thought, this was going to be interesting.

Fast forward to 36 hours later. No longer in the indoor school, but out in the soft, green fields surrounded by stone walls, logs, a coffin jump and various other cross-country excitements. An amused half-smile from Phillips in my direction. 'You lead. We'll follow,' he said.

I eased my calm and confident horse into a canter, allowing him his preference for fast and purposeful work, rolling into a fine, swift rhythm. Jumps taken as part of the whole rolling swing of the thing, nothing to make a drama about. 'Jumping is the art of doing nothing,' Phillips had said at one stage.

Doing nothing, or at least little, I burnt up the course with controlled purpose, halted and waited for the rest. The horse and his rider were, I fear, rather puffed up about it all, but it was the teacher who had the real reason to puff himself up.

And all around were fellow pupils thinking much the same thing.

One woman had never jumped in her life and was confidently tackling chunky obstacles. Every rider was filled with the buzz of achievement.

The fact is that Phillips is not just a born horseman. He is also a born teacher. Teaching is his joy, his special delight, his purpose. Many will recall his inarticulate, fish-out-of-water pronouncements during his period with the big soap. I suggest you forget them. When the subject is horses, Phillips's ability to communicate is a gift.

He can even communicate confidence: to the former non-jumper, to me, to the United States three-day event team. The United States finished tenth at the 1992 Olympic Games, but won the silver medal in 1996. Phillips, their chef d'équipe, gave them purpose, authority, the feeling that they belonged at the high table of world sport.

Phillips likes the company of Americans, perhaps because no American can take the big soap with true seriousness. And, of course, he recently married one, Sandy Pflueger, the (now British-qualified) rider.

American horsepeople are prepared to take Phillips for what he is: a world-class sportsman. You don't expect a world-class sportsman to offer new insights on chaos theory or Marcel Proust. If Phillips is limited, he is limited in the manner of Linford Christie, Steve Redgrave, Ian Botham and Alan Shearer.

Phillips has the CV of a doer, as well as of a teacher; he won gold with the British three-day eventing team at the Munich Olympics in 1972, won Badminton two years running and four times in all. The record is a long way beyond good and, were it not for the big soap, he would be famous only as a top sportsman.

Phillips no longer competes. He is involved in the international horsey life: course design, running the United States team, teaching. He gives riding clinics for paying punters and he is not inclined to take the money and run. The matter of the *Times* man with his borrowed and rackety little animal involved his heart and mind.

His ability to spot and cure a flaw is devastatingly swift. Riding teachers, no doubt because of the military traditions of equestrianism, often parody themselves into hollering martinets. In two days, Phillips never once raised his voice. This is a man on his own ground, confident and generous. This is the man who escaped the big soap and returned to real life and I watched and I took part as real life stamped all around him on pounding hooves.

The Times
22 November 1997

4

The Voice: Sir Peter O'Sullevan

Sir Peter O'Sullevan was not an obvious subject for me: I was trying to write about horses, not about betting and television. But I had always had a hunch about O'Sullevan: and, naturally, I was wrong. Well, I was right about him, but not nearly right enough: he, more than many people more obviously getting their hands dirty in stable yards, could explain what the business of horse racing is really all about.

Racing is sometimes seen as something not really a part of the normal horsey world: a matter of gambling and calculation and form and money. O'Sullevan was always regarded as the punter's man: loving a bet himself, understanding what the betting man seeks from his commentator. But he was driven by far more than love of a gamble. He gets right to the heart of the matter.

People always marvel at the sheer professionalism of Sir Peter O'Sullevan. I can't for the life of me think why. Now it happens that, for reasons best known to itself, *The Times* has asked me to review a book called *Pirelli Calendar Classics*. It is on the floor as I write. I have not the slightest doubt that Kate Moss and Naomi Campbell have the quality of professionalism in overplus: but it is not the first thing that strikes you.

O'Sullevan calls his last race at Newbury this afternoon. He will not make any jokes. He will not make any errors. He will not add any verbal colour at all, but once he has gone, it will seem as if all BBC racing is in monochrome.

He is now in his eightieth year. He has broadcast, on radio or television, on 50 Grand Nationals, 50 Royal Ascots, 50 Goodwoods: nice round figures. And something will go out of racing, out of sport, out of popular culture, with this stepping down.

O'Sullevan represents a genus heading for extinction. He is the voice of his sport. To hear such a voice is (or was) to know exactly where you are, and why. Other members of this genus include John Arlott in cricket, Dan Maskell in tennis, Eddie Waring in rugby league. Others, still living but no longer active, include David Coleman in track and field, and, perhaps, Kenneth Wolstenholme in football.

I doubt if the genus will survive much longer. Modern televised sport – well, there is just so damn much of it, so many competing channels, so many voices clamouring for our attention. The old voices knew they had our attention all along. They never tried, nor needed to try, to seduce. They knew it was a long-term relationship.

O'Sullevan steps down in this year of, as it were, the golden wedding between himself and the viewer and listener. And people will pay due respect to his professionalism, to his ability to pull off the difficult feat of reading a race, remembering all the jockeys' colours and all the names of all the horses.

It is indeed jolly difficult, and I couldn't begin to do it, but a lot of people can. And professionalism isn't exactly unique to O'Sullevan. Professionalism is a minimum expectation. I expect most of us are decent professionals in our way: professionalism is really only absence of vice.

No, the point about O'Sullevan is not his professionalism. It is simply this: love. The reason he possessed the ability to call every race, from the humblest seller to the Grand National, as if it were a matter of all-absorbing interest, was because it was a matter of all-absorbing interest. And you can't fake that.

Every race really is, for the minutes of its running, a matter of fascination. He simply cannot help that quiet relish that is always in his voice as they come under starter's orders, simply cannot help the rise in pitch as the favourite takes it up with a hundred yards to go.

'I'm mad about it,' O'Sullevan said. 'I'm mad about the principal players. And although I'm a punter, the horses always come first.' Every single race is a matter of earth-shattering importance – at least, it is for some of his audience. Some of these will lose money and a few will win. O'Sullevan knows – knows from hard-won experience – that it matters. 'It's all very well for Murray Walker to make cracks and gaffes,' O'Sullevan said. 'The motor-racing audience doesn't have a pecuniary involvement.' He has the respect for a punter that you can only really find in a punter.

A race-reader must be something of an automaton. I was always convinced that the Extel Blower's announcements, before the days of betting-shop television, were made by a Dalek. It was O'Sullevan's triumph to combine such impersonal efficiency with the warmth of an all-too-human punter.

In truth, the myth of O'Sullevan as the world's most fearless punter is somewhat off the pace. 'I don't want to sound clever. I've always bet far too much, far more than I should.' But he sees himself as a cautious punter – and certainly not a gambler, who must bet on every race.

O'Sullevan relishes best the ante-post bet, the taste of the good thing, spotted in humble surroundings, that will soar to ever greater heights. Or not, of course. The romance of the business has never left him. And he has, times without number, commented with his usual impassioned accuracy on races that have carried his money to triumph and disaster, and his voice, always warm, always rising, treating the two imposters just the same.

He managed that, even when he owned the winner himself. And he would mutter, almost swallow the line: Attivo, owned by Peter O'Sullevan, trained by . . . I reminded him of the glorious Michael Bentine record of the football announcer winning the pools and he chuckled – he is one of the few men who can chuckle – for a long time in relish of all the terrible things he didn't do when Attivo, when Be Friendly, strutted their stuff.

In fact, half the tape of our meeting is about Attivo. Which is not really much use to anybody. I have a long series of stories about a terrific horse that was greatly loved. It was, I suppose, rather unprofessional of me to let him run on about how he bought the dam and bred the colt. 'And they said you've got a right little corker here and, if he only grows a little, you'll be able to run him at the White City.'

But the fact is, such horsey tales are the breath of life to those who love talking horse. And, contrary to popular wisdom, hearing them is almost as good as telling them. Like love stories, every horsey tale is the same, and every one is unique. Never mind how he remembers all those different coloured shirts: the love story of O'Sullevan and Attivo is what counts.

'And he won the Daily Express Triumph Hurdle, imagine that, a race sponsored by the newspaper I worked for, and having to make that rather narcissistic announcement at the end.' And he still called every horse home from first to last, without going Michael Bentine. He has a runner, Sounds Fyne, at Newbury this afternoon. Even if it wins, and I hope it does, the usual professionalism will be in place; even if it loses, the warmth of love will still sound in his voice.

He does not plan to shut up completely. He will continue his campaign for something called the air-cushion whip, a device that does not damage the animals. He will also campaign against the live export of horses. Three cheers from this column for both those things.

The pattern runs straight and true, you see. Mad about it. Mad about the game. Above all, mad about horses. From the first pony, best and only friend of an only child, to every horse that has ever run under his assessing eye, he has been mad about them all. Never mind the professionalism. In the end, it is only love that counts.

The Times
29 November 1997

5

A Leg-up on Desert Orchid

Well, I had to write about him, didn't I? Perhaps the best-loved horse ever. A journalist just can't lose with such a subject. But also, as a horseman, you are intrigued: you want to get the feel of a horse who is so impossibly famous.

I have often said to trainers that I would like to visit the yard to interview the horse, rather then the trainer, on account of the fact that horses are more eloquent. This isn't actually true: horses can also be tricky interview subjects. They don't say a lot, after all. The nature of a horse is elusive, and you really need to ride him to get a proper understanding in a short period of time.

Every horse is different, something that comes as a surprise to me every time I sit on the back of a different horse. But capturing it, expressing it in words, is very difficult. Not with Desert Orchid. He had the great public persona of a film star. This is not anthropomorphism: this is a horse with a very big nature. You can't duck it. I venture to suggest it is one of my more rewarding interviews. At least for the interviewer.

A couple of weeks ago, my colleague, Robert Crampton, wrote about a national love object, Ruud Gullit. And he destroyed every preconception about his subject. He wrote that his man was vain, puffed up with self-importance, off-hand, dismissive, impatient and rather ill-mannered.

It is my turn to write about a national love object now: one perhaps more greatly loved, even better-looking and even more conscious of his good looks. The name of the hero is Desert Orchid. I found he was vain, puffed up with self-importance, off-hand, dismissive, impatient and rather ill-mannered.

And, of course, quite wonderful. I punched him lightly on the neck a few times – not a tactic you can work with a footballer – and told him he was a cross old bugger and where were his manners, and put your ears forward and all four paws on the ground.

So, having put me in my place, he took his pat and returned with civilised nose butts. They tell me that he accepts kisses and all kinds of slobbering tokens of affection from his fans on open days. But, right then, he was tacked up and ready to work. This is an animal of quite unique strength of character – you wouldn't expect him to be easygoing. He won races and hearts through his strength and dominant nature. You do not set these things aside just because you've retired.

Boxing Day was ever his day of days, of course, when he won the King George at Kempton more or less as and when he liked, and did so four times in all. Yesterday, he was invited to Kempton to parade before the – his – race. It wouldn't be right not to.

Has any horse in history inspired the love that Dessie did and does? He even has his own fan club, founded when his fame was at its peak. An expert on these matters predicted that it would last two years, and could never outlast the horse's retirement.

The fan club not only survives, it continues to bring in new members. And not racing people, either, still less horsey people. Dessie could not only leap fences, he leapt boundaries of all kinds. He was the horse that united the horsey and the non-horsey worlds.

There is much in Dessie's enduring appeal that is obvious. First, he is a grey – whiter than ever at 18, for as a three-year-old tentatively feeling his way on the Flat, he was the gun-metal grey of James Bond's cigarette case. Horses, like humans, acquire more and more white hairs as they grow older.

Being a grey, and generally the only grey in the race, made him instantly recognisable. Everyone can recognise Dessie. He was also recognisable because he was the one at the front. The place of other horses in Dessie's world is a deferential distance behind. His sense of herd dominance was and is of the incontinent kind: he could not bear to bide his time, not for an instant. But perhaps the true secret of the love that Desert Orchid inspired was his fallibility. His greatness was flawed: and that touched the hearts of his followers as nothing else could.

Red Rum is the only possible rival to Desert Orchid in the race for their love. And Red Rum, with three wins in the Grand National (not to mention two seconds), was arguably the greater racehorse. But Red Rum was about certainty. He did more than seemed possible to remove the element of chance from the great lottery of the National. It was his ability, his uncanny certainty, that was his stock in trade. His racing greatness was, shockingly, unflawed.

But Dessie's flaws were obvious. He could not abide racing left-handed: his trainer, David Elsworth, always reckoned he was a stone better on a right-handed course like Kempton. Cheltenham, of course, is left-handed. Dessie had to race for the Gold Cup, the ultimate accolade, by giving away a stone's advantage. That he won at all is remarkable. His subsequent two thirds probably inspired more affection even than his win.

He never ran in the National. To run or not to run? It was a national debate, nothing less. In a poll, something like 99 per cent of *Daily Mail* readers said that Dessie should not be forced by his 'greedy owners' to take on Becher's and the rest.

'We lost our nerve,' said one of the aforementioned and certainly ungreedy owners, Midge Burridge. 'I mean, what if he had fallen? Or been brought down? What if he had been hurt?' For the question of running or not running the horse was no longer a matter between owner and trainer. The Burridges did not own a horse. They had stewardship of a living national treasure.

And living still, very much so. 'Still pulls your arms out,' Niall Moran, getting a leg-up onto his impatient mount, said. 'Can still get a bit stroppy,' Fay Lucas, who was 'doing' the horse at Elsworth's yard, said.

For Dessie had left his field of mooching retirement and was back with Elsworth for a few weeks to prepare himself for Kempton. And in a fine good temper with himself and the world, too.

There he was, leading out the yearling fillies, daft little tarts of horses skittering and leaping and spooking at the photographer or anything else that caught their eyes. Any excuse.

And there at their head, the big grey, swaggering like Arnold Schwarzenegger. Horses pose. It is an aspect of communication, reading and sending the messages of body language are at the heart of the horsey life – for horses, or for their humans.

And a dominant male strikes poses: tall as he can, puffed up, imposing. On a shallow rise on a grassy plain a posing male can be seen for miles: I am the best horse around. I honestly recommend that you believe that.

All male horses do it: but Dessie does it to the point of self-caricature. He is a horse manifestly conscious of his greatness: he is no three-year-old wet-behind-the-ears classic winner, but a mature individual who, in his way, quietly rages against the dying of the light.

That is perhaps the most endearing trait of all. I sat on his back for a moment, because Elsworth kindly and rightly thought I would like to walk away saying I had done so. I felt pretty tall and proud up there. But he'd expect that.

The Times
27 December 1997

6

Circle of Folly

The gallops at Arundel Castle is one of my favourite places in the world. I once wrote a book on a year in the life of Castle Stables, and a wonderful year it was, mostly because of John Dunlop, the trainer. His generosity not only made the book possible; his generosity was probably the best thing about the book itself.

He is an exceptional man, and I will always be in his debt. I have attempted to repay this by returning to Castle Stables whenever there is a half-decent excuse, to pester John and his staff once again, and enjoy the hospitality of Sue Dunlop.

I had this piece in mind for some time: a piece roughly about the meaning of life, or at least racing. And the only place I could think of to research it – if you can call watching a bunch of lovely horses and talking too much 'research' – was Castle Stables: once again a phone call from me, once again a generous response, once again a beautiful day.

I would like to take this opportunity to say a belated 'happy birthday' to every racehorse in the land. They had their birthday the day before yesterday. Each and every one grew a year older as midnight chimed, corks popped, bad television flooded the airwaves and everywhere people sang incomprehensible songs with bad Scottish accents.

I went to Arundel on New Year's Eve to celebrate this turning of the year, to watch a cavalcade – for once, the word is accurate – of yearlings, 70-odd in all. Sweet-eyed and half-made, they took the last exercise they would have as yearlings. The next day they were out again, each and every one a two-year-old.

Racehorses are born throughout the early months of the year, of course. The 1 January birthday is just a bit of administrative convenience – but rather a dramatic one. It is as if someone had said to these leggy, spooky bundles of nonsense: 'One, two, three and you're a racehorse.'

This is a heart-filling time for anyone who likes horses. Few things are more lovely than a young horse; even people who do not care a jot for horses understand that. And this is a soul-filling time for racing people. Never mind the achievement, feel the potential.

I went to Arundel to visit John Dunlop's racing yard, something of a homecoming for me. Castle Stables lie in the grounds of Arundel Castle, a great park of classically understated English beauty. Aristocratic patronage is no longer the bedrock of racing, but the yearlings, owned by syndicates and sheikhs and smart businessmen and owner-breeders as well as aristocrats, looked the same as ever.

One last yearling was still to be backed and ridden away, a slim chestnut filly working on the long reins and running herself dizzy around her soft-handed lad.

The ground rises steeply from the stable block. At the top of a sharp incline stands a folly. It is a perfect tautology. I stood there on the gallops as a cavalcade of follies skittered past. Every yearling is somebody's folly. Everybody needs a bit of folly in life and horses provide it more generously than most. That is true whether you are a sheikh or the purchaser of a two-quid Tote ticket.

Folly, all is folly. The yearlings come to the yard throughout the autumn, to be backed and ridden away and then to be eased into the hard and thrilling routine of training. No galloping yet, not on those soft, still-growing limbs and soft, still-forming joints. But the horses could now trot up the five-furlong rise and, at halfway, they ease into a nice, cruising canter.

Well, that's the idea. Up they came in small groups, some sensible and settled, some seeking to run for their lives, some twisting and turning and spooking at anything they had a mind to. Stable lads work hard and accept hours and pay that only a madman would envy, but as they ride a green and promising yearling and get the daft little thing working in sudden, proud rhythm, they know that, for a moment, they are richer than any owner in the land.

Stand there beside the canter-track, watch the lad balanced over the withers with his hands giving and taking with soft assurance and see the horse understanding at last what is expected of him. And then watch the low, daisy-cutter stride of the racehorse. A little quotidian bit of magic.

It was at the top of the canter-track, where the horses gather to walk around a nice railed ring beneath proud and ancient trees, that I first heard what can be referred to as Dunlop's Law. To this can be added Stoute's Law, which I was taught on the gallops in Newmarket by Michael Stoute this year as we watched his excellent Pilsudski prepare for his autumn of glories. Between them, the two laws sum up most of Flat racing.

Dunlop's Law tells of the infinite possibilities of folly. 'Any one of these,' he said, pointing to the yearlings a dozen years ago – not dramatically different from the yearlings of 31 December 1997, or for that matter, from the two-year-olds of this morning – 'any one could be, just could be, the greatest racehorse that ever lived.'

He paused: 'They almost certainly won't be. But no one can say certainly that they won't.' This is a beautiful and intoxicating thought.

Stoute's Law is complementary to Dunlop's. I asked him if he was surprised at the apparently endless scope for improvement in Pilsudski. 'You don't get surprises in racing,' he said. 'Just disappointments.'

The two-year-olds I saw are now three-year-olds and three-year-olds are the horses that contest the classics. There, now a freshly minted four-year-old, is the horse that won the St Leger last year and was a fag-paper away from winning the Derby. Silver Patriarch stays in training, to have his tilt at greatness.

The cavalcade left the tree-sheltered ring and descended at a walk back to the stables. The young horses know the routine now. They have a slightly hypnotised, half-cut look to them. Lulled by routine and herd instinct, they walked at their ease.

But it can turn in a flash. One horse spooks and leaps and a domino effect rushes through the herd. The other day three horses got loose and one lad broke his knee. Everybody knows it is crazy to be involved with horses.

And Dunlop recites breeding as the horses file by, sire and dam and dam's sire, a litany of the great. All horsey life is based around the conundrums of nature and nurture. There was one of the last of the foals from that fine stallion, Shirley Heights. Shirley Heights won the Derby from Castle Stables 20 years ago.

Thus racing and the horsey life continue: a feast of perpetual renewal. Each yearling, or now, as we must say, each two-year-old, will have a brief snatch at glory. There will be no surprises, many disappointments. There will be joys and victories and glories. And possibly, just possibly, any one of them – perhaps that noticeably elegant chestnut filly – will be the greatest racehorse that ever drew breath.

She almost certainly won't. But what if she was? We don't know, nobody knows, nobody can know. Thus racing renews itself and the lovely circle of folly is completed again.

The Times
3 January 1998

7

Learning to Be Lester

Every time I have watched a jockey, or a stable lad doing what he does best, I have wanted to have a go. I had always fancied riding jockey style. I used to think it must be so much easier than riding conventionally; years of riding – I really mustn't say 'properly', must I? – had convinced me that changing the habits of a riding lifetime would be very uphill work. But, ever ready to make a fool of myself, I persuaded the British Racing School at Newmarket to leg me up. Look, I really can ride, you know – but in this new style, I was an absolute beginner. Does wonders for your confidence, that does. I'd like to say it taught me to respect stable lads, but I already had a pretty hefty opinion of this eccentric breed. Still, it was great fun, if you don't mind feeling a bit humble.

One difficulty is that although I am riding-fit, it is the wrong

> kind of fitness for this change of method. Another thing is that, all hunched up as you are, it is very hard indeed to get a decent breath. I found the whole thing completely knackering. It was rewarding to try it: and a great pleasure to get back to my own GP saddle at the end of it.

I thought it was my duty as a journalist, and my duty to British racing, to cast my eye over a terribly good-hearted, well-run, well-intentioned scheme for the training of stable staff, the British Racing School in Newmarket.

That is a complete lie, of course. I went there because I wanted to learn to ride like a jockey. I wanted to put my teeth in the mane and my bum in the air; I wanted to perch like an eagle over the withers and feel the great beast roll on beneath me.

'This,' Sue Donnelly said, 'is one of the most demanding of all equestrian disciplines.' I was in no position to disagree, fighting for both my balance and his in an easy canter around the indoor school. 'People talk about dressage and showjumping and eventing. They never consider the skills of people who ride racehorses.'

Well, I consider them. I consider them a very great deal after this visit. And, no, I wasn't really learning to be a jockey. Really, I was learning to be a snotty-nosed little grade D stable lad; minimum wage £91.49. And bloody hell, they have to earn it. And bloody hell, they have some fun while they're doing so.

'Monkeys on sticks chucking whips about.' This summary of the skills required to ride a racehorse rather bears out Donnelly's accusing remark about unconsidered skills. 'Now stop,' Donnelly told me. 'Now shorten your stirrups another four holes.' Up there? You cannot be serious.

The monkeys-on-sticks remark comes from the racing trainer, David Gandolfo, who this week said: 'The racing schools don't cast their nets wide enough. They have this crazy tendency to be looking for potential jockeys as opposed to potential stable staff.'

Well, true, four of the last five champion apprentices come from the school. Royston Ffrench, the present holder of the title, is perhaps the school's most distinguished old boy, though the pigment of his skin tells a reasonably convincing story about wide casting of nets. And he couldn't even ride when he arrived.

They come here for nine weeks, these kids, 16 at a time, and they are guaranteed a job at the end of it. As a stable lad, not a jockey. About 60 per cent of them are female. All must learn the aforementioned unconsidered skills of riding racehorses.

And bloody hell, it is difficult. And I can ride. I have ridden thoroughbreds often enough; in fact, I once reschooled a racehorse into an eventer (admittedly not a very good one) and we collected plenty of rosettes, too.

So I was not in the position of a Ford Escort driver leaping into Michael Schumacher's Ferrari. It was much more difficult than that. It was like leaping into a familiar motorcar and being told that the accelerator, brake and clutch were in a completely different order and, what's more, all up on the dashboard.

A racing saddle is a mere scrap of leather. I never looked on my General Purpose saddles as armchairs before. Ride longer, they have been telling me all my riding life. If you can see your toes, you're wrong. Lower leg down and back: right back behind the girth. Dressage riders ride with the leg almost straight. Riding as I know it, for showjumping, eventing, even polo, are all variations on the same deep seat. But now my leg was bent up at 45 degrees. I was told to bring my leg forward, up to the girth, and if I could not see my toes, I was wrong. Oh, and a touch on the bit does not mean stop, it means go. In fact, in racehorse-riding, just about every command means go.

Racehorses are schooled on the principle of Tom Lehrer's

amoral scientist: 'Vonce ze rockets are up, who cares vair zey come down? Zat's not my department.'

The instruction – Donnelly's not Lehrer's – was very good, very clear, very well thought out. Horse people are supposed to be bad at communication. The opposite is normally the case; in fact everything to do with horses is about communication, mostly across the barrier of species.

Horse people are also very good at communicating with people, so long as the subject is horses and the listener is listening. At the school, some of the kids arrive horsey, but others haven't a clue. Those that listen, listen; those that want to learn, learn. And so they stay and go on to their jobs in the racing industry.

I listened too, I learnt. And there were moments of pure joy, short moments of considerable joy, as I clicked, and had horse and self balanced. And then the extraordinary unnatural shortness of the stirrup leathers suddenly made sense.

And then unfitness and unfamiliarity would undo me and, cursing myself, I sought balance once again. This riding technique is a very specific skill and one not lightly gained. Those that can do it right should be cherished.

And there is more cherishing of stable staff than there used to be, that is for sure. And more money. There is even a career structure: a grade A lad gets a minimum of £196.41. 'Two a penny, you lot,' one stable lad once said to me. 'That's what the trainer said to me. Two a penny!'

Not any more. There is – well, not a crisis in stable staff, but at least recognition that good staff are hard to get and hard to keep. And worth getting and worth keeping. Even in racing, feudalism is no longer an option.

It is compulsory for all new racing staff to attend the school, or the other school in the North. The qualification is a genuine one, universally recognised. The school is backed with government money. It is a tough nine weeks of constant appraisal and necessary self-examination. The hours are cruel. It is, therefore, a realistic preparation for real life in a racing stable. Mucking out and grooming are every bit as important as riding, though I was lucky enough to be let off those bits.

Qualification from the school is a bit like giving up cigarettes. The secret is really wanting to do it. The rewards are obvious, at least, they are to anybody who has sat on a horse. Every day, twice a day, teeth in the mane, bum in the air, beast moving sweetly beneath you, horse and human in perfect balance – if you are good enough. Your unconsidered skills are most unlikely to earn you a fortune.

As in all sport, all kids are in a turtles-and-the-sea situation. Who appreciates these hard-won, unconsidered skills? Good trainers do. And so do good horses. Stable lads are richer than the common run of humankind – at least, they are for a couple of hours in each day.

The Times
21 February 1998

8

On the Cutting Edge with Martin Pipe

Martin Pipe is one of the more formidable obstacles a horsey journalist can take on. All sports tend to pretend they are cosy worlds full of mutual admiration: call it the Our Great Game Syndrome. But National Hunt does this more than any other. It likes to offer a picture of itself as the world's cosiest and most clubbable sport.

Pipe, neither cosy nor clubbable, has changed the way people think and work in National Hunt racing. It has made him widely disliked, and the dislike makes him very self-protective. He is always very friendly: and not given to easy trust.

He is very approachable, polite, easy to talk to: hard to get him to give anything away. He has been right so many times that people think there must be something wrong about him.

No doubt about it, it was one of the great sights of the horsey year. Martin Pipe's horses for Cheltenham: here they come! In a great rolling wave, a great rolling canter, stable lads and the champion jockey moving forward as one. And the horses; oh, such horses, on up the steep Devonian slope and back down again.

Martin Pipe's horses for Cheltenham: is there a trainer in the land who wouldn't swap his entire string for a half of these, or a quarter? Quality through and through. Martin Pipe's horses for Cheltenham: they seemed to take about ten minutes to go past, and they were going a fair clip, too.

The champion goes to the championship, for the Cheltenham Festival sends racing into its annual, shuddering three days of ecstasy on Tuesday. And the Pipe stable takes part with the massive condescension, massive resources and the massive ambition of Manchester United.

No one likes us, we don't care. Like Alex Ferguson, the United manager, Pipe is convinced that the world is against him. And, like Ferguson, Pipe is more or less exactly half right. And, like Ferguson, he is adept at using the thick streak of paranoia to the greatest possible advantage of his team.

The team: because the lads are all in team colours, Pipe sweatshirts and Pipe windcheaters, just as the horses are all in Pipe exercise sheets. Or not so much a team: Pipe has made Nicolashayne, in Devon, a kind of personal company town.

Why does no one, or, rather, only half of the world, like Pipe, like the Pipe team? For let us get one fact straight: Pipe is an absolutely magnificent trainer of racehorses. You don't become a serial champion trainer by fluke, still less by skulduggery.

And I sat in his kitchen after the horses had returned to the yard, eating an egg kindly and deftly fried at the Aga by Carol Pipe, reading a clipping that happened to be on the table. Laser technology. A claim that lasers can repair torn ligaments and ruptured tendons. More technology: naturally Pipe is interested.

And suddenly, I was not in a nice kitchen at a thriving racing yard. I was in the Williams racing-car factory when they were right at the very top of Formula One. Voracious for technology. The intense, forbidding presence of Frank Williams, passionate for victory; passionate for anything that will give an edge over the rest.

That's Formula One. With the Williams edge now gone, the technological advantage lies with McLaren. But here at the Pipe pits, Pipe still has the edge. And he is as voracious for technology as ever: he intends to keep that edge.

In Formula One, team dominance comes and goes and returns. Pipe continues to shrug off the challengers, and the more he does so, the more he is resented. You are just not supposed to be that good, not in the gentle, jolly, sporting sport of National Hunt racing, when it's all jolly good luck and let's hope the horse comes back sound.

Actually, it never was like that, not at the sharp end of the sport; it never is like that at the sharp end of any sport.

Perhaps Pipe's crime was that he shattered the pretence. He brought the real world into the sport of National Hunt racing. Or, worse, he made it clear that the real world had been part of the lovely game all along.

Punters are romantic; perhaps none more romantic than the real hard-nut, who is romantic about money, romantic about wagering, romantic about his own dream of personal toughness. Bookmakers are not romantic. If I toss a coin with you for a quid and you win, I will give you a quid. Toss coins with a bookmaker, and he will give you 5–4 on heads, 5–4 on tails. And keep the change.

If you and I toss coins over a statistically meaningful period, we will end up even. By the same rule, a bookmaker will end up with rather a lot of money. That is the difference between them and us. By astute calculation, they eliminate the element of chance from a business that is based on chance.

Pipe is a bookmaker by nature and nurture, a bookmaker's son. He has done his damnedest to eliminate chance from the chancy business of training racehorses: and he has come nearer to succeeding than any trainer that has ever existed. No wonder his rivals hate him.

I had been to the Nicolashayne stables before, of course. I knew the story that his priority, perhaps even before the looseboxes, was to establish a swimming pool, and a laboratory. The blood-testing of horses is part of the daily routine. Run him when his blood is right; never dream of running him when it is wrong.

Blood-testing is part of racehorse training everywhere, but at Pipe's it is obsessive. But then so is everything. The solarium, for horses to sunbathe after their swims. X-ray equipment, scopes for tendons, scopes for the lungs. Pipe owns every bit of technology that might work. New since my last visit was a loose-jumping ring, in which a horse can learn to jump without the inconvenience of a rider on his back.

'He asks questions of tradition,' Peter Scudamore, former stable jockey and, therefore, former champion jockey, said. The two jobs tend to go together. Pipe really is that good. An obsessive man; also, a man carrying a deep wound.

There have always been unsubstantiated stories about Pipe's methods. There was even a television programme dedicated to exposing Pipe as monster. Nothing was proved except the world's relentless mistrust of an outsider's success.

For Pipe has always been an outsider in racing's cosy world: first as a bookmaker's son, then as a trainer based not in matey, scandal-ridden Lambourn, but miles away in Devon. 'You can't train from there, old boy.'

He didn't have it in the blood, didn't set about it in the right way. Those endless victories of his have been unforgivable; and remain unforgiven. Not surprising that the more winners he had, the more frenetic Pipe seemed to get: always friendly, never letting anyone get in close. Speedy, twitchy, always on edge. And always winning.

They say, well, Pipe is all very well for a nice touch at Newton Abbot. But what about the big races? Pipe has won the lot now, all save the Gold Cup. And is genuinely mellower now. Still strung up, of course, but more like a cello than a violin these days.

A degree of acceptance, perhaps. Knowing that genuine excellence and poisonous envy are inseparables; that the one thing people hate more than a tradition-breaker is a tradition-breaker who succeeds. Lets the whole side down, that, makes us all look like fools.

Pipe knows these things now, knows also that smart punters and a good few owners love him, and knows that the flow of winners will not dry up. He has never stopped caring, but he has been able to ease up just a fraction on the worrying. And, as for that Gold Cup: it will come. Maybe even on Thursday.

One final thought: one of the best-loved horses in racing history was the uncompromising Red Rum, the horse who turned the greatest lottery in national life into something approaching a certainty. Martin Pipe: Red Rum without the love.

The Times
14 March 1998

9

A Brief Guide to Breeding a Champion

A race does not begin when the starter says go. It begins years earlier, in the dramatic encounter between stallion and mare. I have a theory about sport – well, I have many, but one will do for now. And that is that all sports are metaphors: normally a battle, or a duel, though cricket is also a metaphor for life and death.

Racing, I once thought, was too simple a matter to be a metaphor for anything: you just run the race and then you either win it or lose it. But racing is not just the race: it is everything; and it starts with the meeting in the breeding shed. And I realised that racing is in fact a metaphor for evolution: only the best, the most suitable, go on to breed. Only the best become ancestors. Here are three pieces on the mysteries of breeding: two from *The Spectator*, and one in the middle from *The Times*.

MYSTERIES WITHIN MYSTERIES

Mysteries within mysteries within mysteries. That sums up everything to do with horses; but the greatest mystery of all is breeding. I have always loved the phrase 'a horse he bred himself' as if the top-hatted owner had really been involved in the rearing and the plunging.

You might think that breeding a nice horse was reasonably straightforward. You get a Derby winner for the dad and an Oaks winner for the mum, prepare the bridal suite, and four years on you watch their offspring win the Derby. And that is exactly how it was for Lammtarra.

Lammtarra (by Nijinsky out of Snow Bride, if you care) runs in the Prix de l'Arc de Triomphe in Paris on Sunday, having picked up this year's Derby and the King George V already. If only everything in life and horses were as simple.

I have been reading a venerable book by the Italian breeder Federico Tesio, *Breeding the Racehorse*, a book that tells of a lifetime's struggle to bring logic to bear on the eternal mysteries of breeding horses. A remarkable man, Tesio anticipated, in 1935, what is considered the most astonishing innovation in racing.

This is the Godolphin method, by which Lammtarra, among others, has been nurtured to brilliance. That southward instinct – do we feel it too, as human animals, when the summer dies on its feet all around us? Do we long to warm our bones in the dry heat of southern lands? Even Dubai?

Tesio writes of horses: 'Were they free like bison, they too would journey south, guided by their craving and their sixth sense.' And so Sheikh Mohammed has taken to moving his best young horses south to Dubai, where they take to themselves the power of the sun. Tesio moved his horses more modestly as far south as Sicily, and thus produced his greatest horses, Donatello and Nearco.

All very logical. But in the end, all is mystery. I get letters from Weatherby's, the horse registration people, addressed to 'Dear breeder'. I am indeed a registered breeder. I bred a single horse 'myself', though I claim no active part where it mattered. I did help the foal out into the blackness of night three years ago, but that is another story.

How do you choose a sire for your mare? I had so much advice on this mystery I almost gave up. 'But whatever you do, do not put your mare to the first stallion you set eyes on.' So, of course, I put my mare to the first stallion I set eyes on. I knew he was perfect, and I was right.

And lucky. In the end, no matter how much logic you start with, there comes a moment when you must surrender to the eternal mystery of the horse. Tesio tells of Cavaliere Ginistrelli, an Italian about Newmarket in 1904. He was leading his prized and beloved mare – she and Ginistrelli had adjoining sleeping quarters – Signorina through the streets of the town to her tryst with the stallion of his choice.

At the time, it was the custom to parade lowly stallions around Newmarket, touting their wares. And on Signorina's journey she met just such a low-caste beast, one Chaleureux. 'Chaleureux at once proved worthy of the name,' Tesio writes. 'He gave signs of a violent infatuation. Signorina looked upon him with equal favour and also refused to move on. No amount of tugging or pleading had any effect.

'Ginistrelli sized up the situation at a glance. "They love!" he exclaimed. "A love match it shall be."' The result of this love was a filly called Signoretta, who won the Derby and then, two days later, the Oaks: perhaps the greatest race filly of all time.

Naturally enough, the lovers had their chance to meet again. They produced another beautiful filly. She was called Star of Naples. She raced until she was five and never won a race. And no doubt the Arc will be won by some no-account whose sire I have never heard of.* Moral: horses can discomfort even sheikhs. No one else would dare.

The Spectator
30 September 1995

A NIGHT AT THE NATIONAL STUD

Spring. The Cheltenham Festival celebrates the end of winter, but down on the stud, they celebrate the beginning of the season of birth, of growth, of life. They have been celebrating it since January and knackered, flat out, utterly caught up in their world of quotidian miracles, they will go on celebrating it until the end of June.

The Flat season starts next Thursday, and off we go for another round of disaster and joy. These two ingredients are mixed in proportions of approximately twenty to one, but the second does rather go to your head. And as we wait to hear the first cuckoo, so experienced watchers of the Flat are looking out for the spring's first Horse of the Century.

And, damn me, here was a Horse of the Century: neck of a bull on him now, and Schwarzenegger shoulders. He was all elegance and grace on the racecourse, but he was merely a boy then. Now he is all swagger and shove and the very antithesis

* Lammtarra, of course, won brilliantly.

of hallo-horsey-have-a-Polo. Not nasty: just a stallion in his pomp.

You tell a gelding, the old horsey saying goes, and you ask a mare. With a stallion, well, you talk things over. This was Celtic Swing, Horse of the Century just three years ago, a very good horse who, in the end, was still a fag-paper away from greatness. All the same, a date with this hard-muscled, head-tossing beast will cost his admirers £6,500 a go.

I was at the National Stud, a 500-acre dream factory hard by the July Course in Newmarket, there to spend 24 hours listening to the rite of spring. Where better to go in Cheltenham week?

Money and winners. Winners and money. There is a theory that this is what Flat racing is all about. Many of the horsey world's legion of non-racing people believe it. So do many others. Indeed, many racing people believe it. I have a theory that they are all wrong and that the racing people who believe their game is only about victory are deluding themselves.

To believe that racing is not really about winning is a very serious heresy, I know. But walk from the stallions' line, where the lowering, bull-necked pashas await the next luscious mares that have been procured for them, down to the paddocks, greenswards and post-and-rail fencing, where graze the mares. And foals.

Is there a person in existence who can look at a fortnight-old foal without a lifting and a softening of the heart? If so, this person has had his humanity surgically removed. A foal represents the lowest common denominator of sentimentality. Ridiculous legs. Foals have to buckle at the knees like a drinking giraffe to get a mouthful of grass. Bravely leaving their mother's side for seconds and more at a time, then beginning to socialise. Silly bouncing games, and then the sudden foal's flop of perfect exhaustion, flat on the ground with legs stretching a ridiculous distance from silly little bodies.

Celtic Swing was like that once, and so was Hector Protector and the other seven stallions that stand at the National Stud. Any of the present crop of flopping bundles might be as good or better. But who cares? On a hard, cold, sun-filled morning, a mistle thrush singing behind the field, it is hard to think about anything except now. Here are mares, and here are foals, and that is more than enough.

Racing tries its damnedest to be a tough, ruthless business, but it keeps failing. The trouble is that horses keep getting in the way.

Mares come to the stud to visit a stallion. But, mostly, they arrive full of the foal they conceived last year, for the gestation period is 11 months. And so the foals are born at the stud, and shortly after the birth, the mares come into season and meet the stallion of their owner's latest dreams.

So a stud is not, after all, a place dominated by the bull-necked swaggerers; not, after all, a shrine to the male principle. A stud is an intensely female place: stout, waddling and gravid, an atmosphere hippy and bosomy. Birth dominates the daily processes: copulation, the purpose of the enterprise, almost a sideshow.

Everywhere you look there are pregnant mares, and mares and foals. Everywhere, horses growing inside and outside mares. Every night the watchers watch, for mares almost always foal under cover of darkness, an atavistic response to the no-longer-existent threat of predators.

No wolves: only vets and lavish foaling pens and every aid that technology can give them. But this is still a profoundly atavistic business. Mares, fat and round and itching with discomfort, awaiting the final moment. Then the sweating, stamping, brief and terrible drama of birth. I cannot see a pregnant mare without remembering the spring night when I sat with a seconds-old foal in my lap, wet, slithering and snorting fluid. My mare, my foal, now a strapping great git of 17 hands.

That daily impossibility: now there is one, and now there are two. The greatest miracle of all, happening here at the National Stud at a pace that is almost relentless. Tragedy, too, for a foal was killed in an accident. It may not be tragedy to you, but the mare was left overnight with the little corpse to sniff and puzzle over; normally a mare buries a dead foal in the straw. A mare will recover quicker if she is given the opportunity to grieve.

Money and winners, is it? Try putting a price on the gloom that fell over the place when the foal received the death sentence. Estimate the guilt people feel when they know there is nothing more they can do and nothing more they could have done. Life happens; so does death.

But where there is life there is hope, and where there is hope there are wild and impossible dreams. That, not victory, is racing's stock-in-trade. Life: hope: dreams.

Afternoon at the stallion yard. Mare calm, receptive, ready. Stallion in a sudden ecstasy of excitement. The stallion man holding the entire life force of the planet on the end of a thin bit of leather, but he was as calm and matter-of-fact as a person could be at this earthy and earth-moving encounter.

A-squealing and a-mounting, the mare ringing like a drum at the amorous clasp of the stallion's fore-limbs, vast yellow teeth sinking into her neck, protected by a leather cape from monstrous love-bites. And then it's all done. Good boy. Well done, darlin'.

Vet's round in the post-dawn chill. A sickly foal is at least alive and sucking hard. Next, a first-timer, a no-longer-maiden filly. Enigmatic screen of the scanner. 'Yyyyup.' What? Where? 'There.' A pale fleck inside a dark fleck: life. A spark of life: a foal. Another horse, another miracle, another dream.

I'm right, you know. Winning is part of it. But winning is not the reason. It is just the excuse, The real reason is dreaming. All around us, dream creatures moved and worked their daily miracles.

The Times
21 March 1998

FRAILTY, THY NAME IS HORSE

I am writing these words in the most terrible sulk. Entrepreneur did not win the Derby, you see. And it really is most frightfully unfair, because I much wanted him to. Perhaps a cynical sneer, perhaps an understanding smile rises to your lips: how much, you wonder, did the silly bugger bet? How much did he lose?

The answer is, not a penny. The silly bugger has far more efficient means of disposing of money by means of horses than mere betting; they are called livery bills and farrier's bills and vet's bills. No, I felt a far keener disappointment than the sort obtainable with mere money.

Racing is, of course, about disappointment. To be a punter is to place yourself in a situation of being a permanent, long-term loser. You don't have to be Sigmund Freud or, for that matter, Albert Einstein to work that out. The entire notion of odds is purposefully designed to make sure that a steady trickle or flood of money flows from punter to bookie. It is a matter of financial gravity.

'I am a peddler of dreams,' said Miles Littlewort, chief executive of the National Stud, when I paid a recent visit there to rub the noses of hours-old foals, to slap the muscled necks of stallions, to get nibbled to death by yearling fillies. There is something perverse in making horses the vehicle for your dreams. 'Frailty, thy name is Sceptre!' moans Lenehan in *Ulysses* as his sure-fire certainty for the Ascot Gold Cup of 16 June 1904 gets beaten by the dark horse Throwaway. Frailty, thy name is Entrepreneur. Frailty, thy name is thoroughbred. Frailty, thy name is horse.

'How are your beasts?' I asked a racing owner at the Derby. 'One's very slow, one's very lame.' I rang my sister: 'How's that new mare?' 'Had to sell it at a loss. Quite unmanageable.' I rang a friend, the top dressage rider Debi Thomas. She can't get to the phone: she's lame – foot and ankle got mangled by a horse.

There is a notion that people love horses because they have power over them. Nothing could be further from the truth. Horses have power over people: power over their imaginations, power over their dreams. The British suffer from this to a greater extent than most. British car stickers boast of willingness to eat mad cows. The British eat hamburgers almost incessantly, a hamburger being a device to make every single bit of cow more or less digestible. But eat a horse? We'd rather die. It's cannibalism.

Taboo – nothing less. There is something atavistic about the British feeling about horses: the relish or the horror with which bad falls at the Grand National or Badminton are received, the terrible sadness and anger that greets the news of a horse killed on a big sporting occasion.

At Epsom, before the Derby, it was the opposite, a feeling of joy and hope. The myth of greatness was about to be played out in front of us. We were about to set our eyes on the miracle that one horse, as Sherlock Holmes put it, could run faster than another. The race, it seemed, was not a three-pipe problem: Entrepreneur would hack up and become the greatest since Nijinsky, the greatest horse this century, the greatest horse since Eclipse, the greatest horse ever.

Greedy for greatness, I did not necessarily believe, but I hoped. After all, I saw him win the Guineas, and I saw him parade before the Derby, gleaming, the handsomest thing on four legs you have ever seen. 'It will be Eclipse first, the rest nowhere.' That was the confident and utterly accurate eighteenth-century prediction. Well, I thought, Entrepreneur will eclipse every other horse in Epsom. But in the end, the sun set in the west, water continued to run downhill, money still flowed from punters to bookies, and Entrepreneur was just another horse, just another dream. Ah well, there'll be another one along in a minute. Do you want to know what my young horse did last week?

The Spectator
14 June 1997

10

Stable Lads: a Race of Heroes

Phil Sharp became a hero when he refused to be evacuated during the great Aintree bomb scare, and stayed behind to look after the horses. If this sounds brooding and tough and intense, it is nothing like Sharp: as easy and as amiable a person as you could meet, one of those people who seem in constant good temper, the kind that keeps a yard sane on winter mornings.

Some doubted Sharp's sanity after his adventure, but his is a madness that we British like very much. Indeed, there is a little of Sharp in every horsey person: but Sharp was the one who did it. This is a celebration of Sharp. I follow this up with a piece from *The Spectator* celebrating all his colleagues as well.

THE LAD WHO STAYED BEHIND

Oh, we British and our horses, eh? Every year on Grand National weekend, we are filled with a complacent delight in our own madness. And the rest of the world watches and wags its head in dismay. Sont fous, ces Britanniques!

No one is untouched by the madness. Even those remote from the event nod self-approvingly. Those that oppose the race still revel in being British archetypes: caring more for the poor horses than their owners. The British weep for what the French eat.

This is an annual weekend of horsey love. Love of hazard, love of spectacle, love of Britishness, for this race is British in a way that the Derby and the Cheltenham Gold Cup cannot begin to challenge. And love, of course; love of horses, whether you love the race or hate it.

Which brings us to bombs, and to Phil Sharp, the hero of Aintree. Sharp is an archetype of British life. He is like the man who paints the Forth Bridge. He is like Swampy: a person who fulfils a national need.

Sharp is the Lad Who Stayed Behind. As the coded warning came in at the Grand National last year, Aintree was evacuated, leaving behind the horses. And Phil, somehow overlooked, as stable lads tend to be. Staying behind, the boy on the burning deck, whence all but he had fled, seeing to the horses, 50 of them. Rather more than doing your two, as racing jargon has it.

Sharp looked after the burly and well-fancied grey, Suny Bay. He still does. Nothing has changed, after his brief 15 minutes, and doubtless nothing will change after its brief recapitulation this year. Nothing bar a few teases from his colleagues in a profession notoriously long on banter.

I met him briefly when I went to interview Suny Bay a few weeks ago. 'Never knew there was a bloody bomb,' Charlie Brooks, Suny Bay's trainer and Sharp's guv'nor, said. 'What bomb? he said. Couldn't work out where all the other buggers had got to.'

And Sharp smiled tolerantly enough, no doubt only the five hundredth time he had heard this joke. I don't really remember his face; my eyes were all for the horse. Which is the way of things for stable lads. And, well, Suny Bay was and is a terrific horse, carries top weight today, and Sharp will travel up with him and groom him until he gleams – not easy with a grey, that – and until his tail flows like a million strands of silk. And he will tack him up and walk him in hand till he turns him over to the jockey, and the horse will look several million dollars and will turn every head on the racecourse and no one will notice Sharp at all.

Of course, Sharp is a wonderful symbol, a perfect imagination-catcher. He defied the terrorists, but he also defied the police. He defied both danger and the law, which adds a certain subversiveness to his heroics: a Robin Hood for horses.

And lest we think that the whole thing was blown out of all proportion, there was some real point to Sharp's defiance. There would have been injured and probably dead horses without him. The horses were abandoned in all their tack, according to police instructions. One horse had already rolled and got his legs hopelessly tangled in his reins. This is the time for a horse to panic and break a leg.

And panic spreads through a herd of horses at the speed of

light, whether they are roaming wild on the plains or standing in a row of looseboxes. Sharp untangled, calmed, patted, untacked the whole lot of them, made much of all of them, watered and hayed them.

'I don't think the police realised we were still there,' Sharp said. 'But it wouldn't have made any difference because I wouldn't have left the horses.' His wife, Gail, said that when she heard there was one stable lad left behind, she had no doubts as to who it was.

Sharp is now 33 and has three children. The word 'lad' does not mean boy. The job of stable lad now has a proper wage structure and their skills are recognised, if not recklessly over-rewarded. It is a hard job, physically demanding and requiring the high skills of riding out two, sometimes three, times a day.

And it has its riches all right, and the fierce, controlled gallops of work mornings are just part of them. The job is about involvement: the deep relationship that no person can avoid if he spends many hours of the day in the sole company of another sentient being.

For Suny Bay is Sharp's horse. Uplands Bloodstock may think that they own him. Brooks may think that, as trainer, he owns him. His jockey, Graham Bradley, certainly has an important relationship with him and so does Mel Gurdon, the equine physiotherapist who has worked so hard in Suny Bay's preparation.

But the only true owner is Sharp, who has no say in the horse's destiny. Suny Bay may be the favourite horse of Uplands Bloodstock, or Brooks, or Bradley. But Sharp is Suny Bay's human of choice: and that is glory enough to be going on with.

I know that you think me daft, the way I go on about

horses and the relationships between horses and humans. I try to explain what it is like to be committed to a horse, or horses. I try to explain, knowing that I am describing colour to the blind.

But those of us with horsiness in our blood know that Sharp's great adventure was, in a sense, no great shakes. Not that we would all have done it, all have stayed behind. We do not, any of us, know how we will act at any moment of truth.

But certainly most of us would have wanted to stay: and practically all of us would have wished that we had done so. Not when we found out how it all turned out, but about 30 seconds after we had accepted the police instructions and discovered there was no way back.

Sharp himself said: 'I can't believe all the fuss that was made. I found myself in a position where I was the only one who could look after the horses. Anyone involved with racing would do the same.'

And apart from changing the word 'racing' to 'horses', I agree with every word. Perhaps any horsey person would have done it: but the point is that Sharp actually did do it. Which means that, first of all, he stands for the horsey people of Britain, all us nutcases for whom a day without horses is a day without the sun.

But also Sharp stands for all the vicariously horsey people of Britain, the legions who love from afar, those who love the Grand National and those who hate it.

Sharp stands for the grand and the national love of horses: soft-hearted, foolish, defiant of logic and common sense. Last year, on a weekend in which terror was avoided by a hair's breadth, we celebrated the daft, defiant love of a man for his horse and for horsekind.

Would you have stayed? That is the great, the several-million-dollar question. But we would all have wanted to. Sharp stands for the bit in us all that wanted to stay. But he also stands for the bit in himself that actually did.

The Times
4 April 1998

RACING FOR LOVE

Racing often calls itself an industry rather than a sport. Perhaps so, but it is a pretty rum one. For a start, it is the only industry I know which is totally dedicated to providing money for another industry – the book-making industry. Racing, at a pivotal point in its history, was too grand to sully its fingers with sordid trade, and so it must exist without controlling its betting money, and it is the betting money that turns the industrial wheels.

The sport or industry depends entirely on subsidy, and the owners are always picked out as the principal subsidisers. There are also the sponsors and the bookmakers, who pay a levy into the industry. The point is that owners are in it for one thing: love. Can an industry be run entirely on love?

It costs at least £10,000 a year to have a racehorse in training. The sheikhs have hundreds of them all over the world, others pay the dues of their love by being members of a syndicate, and they count themselves lucky if the damn thing ever gets to a racecourse. But love is not about satisfaction. Love is only about love – such things as satisfaction, gratification and even pleasure are bonuses.

Love envelops the whole demented edifice of racing. The Glorious Goodwood festival of the past week is one more tribute to the enduring love that dominates the business; a love that is often corrupted, perverted, jealous, ruinous, obsessive, self-aggrandising, self-punishing, depraved, unhealthy, all-consuming, absurd, ridiculous, mad – but love can be all those things, separately, serially, simultaneously. Neither racing nor love has very much to do with rationality.

Those who analyse the industry are aware of these things, aware that the business is founded on the rock of the owner's irrational love of glory, horses, chances, disappointment, whatever. But they tend to miss the point that the industry is also subsidised at the bottom end. The stable lads are, just as much as the owners, subsidising racing. They, just as much as the owners, are in it for love.

Their love is a difficult way of life. The hours are killing and the pay is small. The work is highly dangerous: half a ton of overfed, neurotic, brainless two-year-old is not always amenable to polite negotiation. Working conditions are hard: the military traditions of the game make for a rigid and often uncomfortable hierarchy. The life is halfway between appalling and so enviable you wonder why everybody doesn't do it. Hard, bright mornings, hard, bright, wild horses, and twice a week the sudden vicious gallops. The care, the secret shared knowledge, and, as ever, the quest for victory and the thrill of the punt.

No need to romanticise them. Racing yards have their share of skivers, drinkers, out-of-control gamblers, nutters and bores. Lads are, to a man, to a woman, grumblers, just like everybody else in every other industry. Most of them are also thoroughly decent sorts, most of them are ridiculously brave, and most of them can ride like Cossacks.

No need to feel sorry for them, for they get a better deal than the owners on the whole. The owners only get the prize money and the glory. The lads get the horses and, on those rare and glorious moments when the beast passes the post in front of all the others, they have a greater right than the owner to say, 'Look, my horse won.' Like the owners, they know that the business and their involvement in it are colossal folly. Unlike the owners, they give not their money, but their time: days, weeks, months, years, lives. Who was it that said non-obsessive love is like alcohol-free lager?

The Spectator
2 August 1997

11

Mark Todd: the Best Ever

This piece may come over as being too admiring. If so, I have done the job right. Mark Todd is, simply, the best I have ever seen, in any horsey discipline. I remember in the press-room of some three-day event or other, when someone, in good quotes-pooling fashion, reported back that, though the riders in general thought the course was very tough, Todd said it would flow.

There was a general snort at this. 'All courses flow if you're Mark Todd,' somebody said. They do. There is an illusion you see sometimes when Todd is riding: it is as if all the fences had been lowered 12 inches into the ground for his approach, and then raised again for everybody else.

Horsey people talk about 'seeing a stride', that ability to make your final adjustment in approach a long distance away from the fence. Todd sees a stride from a mile off.

I never had the chance to watch Shakespeare write, so I don't know if it's true that he never blotted a line. Did he look out of the window for hours between sentences? Did he scribble frenziedly when the words came? Did he go back and improve, did he get stuck, or was it all ridiculously easy?

I would love to know, not because it would give me a few hints on improving my working method, but – well, being a chap who writes a bit himself, it would just be nice to watch. Ha, I would say. I do that. True, the results are different. But it's what I do.

Never mind. I may not have watched Shakespeare write, but I have watched Mark Todd school a horse. I watched Todd and I thought, ha. I do that. True, the results are different. But it's what I do.

The gap in class is about the same in each case. This is not being humble. It is audacious and ridiculous for any writer to speak of himself and Shakespeare in the same sentence. Same with horse riders and Todd.

No writer envies Shakespeare. You can only admire. It is the same with Todd and riders. He is the best competitive horseman practising at present, perhaps the best ever. Francome? Shoemaker? You could argue a case for either against Todd. But you would lose.

Todd is a three-day eventer. A three-day eventer is always defined as a Jack of all trades, master of one. The Jack part is dressage, showjumping, endurance and steeplechase; the master part is cross-country, the testing to the limit of horse and rider over the most fiendish and terrifying obstacles that man can devise.

The definition works for every three-day eventer that ever took on the ultimate challenge of horsemanship. But not for Todd. Impossibly, he is master of them all. He could be international class in any one discipline. I need only tell one story to prove this point for all time. I will tell it in a moment, but bear with me. I spent a day watching Todd at work at his base on the far rim of the Thames watershed. He has 25 horses in his string and he schools up to eight in a day.

This is not because he finds it hard to delegate. It is because delegation is not an option. Three-day eventing is designed to test (to the limit) the understanding, the trust between horse and rider. And this is something that takes years, not months to establish.

Flashback to Badminton 1991. Badminton, the ultimate test in the ultimate horsey sport, the ultimate examination of the understanding between rider and horse. A couple of days before the competition began, a rider was injured. The horse, trained to the minute, was without a pilot.

So they asked Toddy. A chance ride round Badminton? Where even the dressage is an ordeal, even when you are on your own horse? Sure, said Toddy. And so Todd got on Horton Point for the first time in the middle of Badminton week, and – ridiculous, isn't it? – rode the horse to victory.

You're just not supposed to be able to do that. If any other rider had done it, we would all have wondered if all the guff about bonds between horses and riders was utter nonsense. It would have been as if the pretensions of the sport had been laid bare. Yet the sport has no pretensions. This was just the Todd factor. There was no need to question the sport, only to salute the finest piece of competition riding in the history of equestrian competition.

So that's Toddy. Long, lean New Zealander, standing six foot three inches. Two individual Olympic golds, three Badmintons, four Burghleys and a little weariness behind the eyes, not so much from the 42 years as from the recent death of his friend, David

Foster,* after a fall at an event in Ireland. This is a hard and dangerous life, let no one forget.

And that's me, watching Todd's school. First, two eight-year-olds, longish-range possibles for the Sydney Olympic Games of 2000. A frustrating, talented chestnut, a grey with a better mind but a mite less spark. And Todd, tuning in to Radio Station Equus. As ever.

What did I learn for my own use? Sad to say, absolutely nothing. What did I understand, so that I can pass it on to the readers of this column? Sad to say, very little. Why is Shakespeare so great? Because he has a nice choice of words. Why is Todd so great? Because he has good balance. He never looks big on a horse; odd, when there is so much of him to dispose about an animal. He possesses to a very high degree the ability to move hands, arms and legs independently and with immense precision, while being bucketed about on board a moving conveyance. Quite stunning physical coordination, which partly comes from his superb balance.

'And you should see him play squash,' one of his grooms said. 'Not just the coordination. The competitive instinct.' Reins rather longer than is conventional. Not the guardsman straight back, either: a kind of lanky Red Indian slouch in the saddle. The contact a feather, if that.

Contact? This is horsey jargon, meaning the amount of pressure that the hand puts through the reins on to the bit, the principal line of communication between horse and human. I have never seen such effective riding from so minute, so trifling a contact. If the bit were cobweb, Todd would not break it. 'Self-balance,' Todd said. 'A horse must never rely on his rider for balance.' It is riders who make horses fall. Loose horses do not fall and seldom clout

* This was written before the dreadful year of 1999, in which five event riders were killed.

an obstacle. This is one of the oldest – and most humbling – rules of horsemanship.

Like all the great secrets of the world, the secret of Mark Todd's horsemanship is that there is no secret. He does exactly the same as the rest of us. Just better, that's all. Oh, and since you ask, he is as decent a fellow as you could meet in a day's march. So that's it. Do I sound sycophantic? Gushing? Over the top? Then good. That is exactly what I intended. But it is time to get a little perspective. A little context. How good is Mark Todd?

Literature: Shakespeare, Joyce, Dante, Homer. Postwar sport: Ayrton Senna, Carl Lewis, Michael Jordan, Martina Navratilova, Sir Garfield Sobers, Pele, Steve Redgrave. And Mark Todd.

The Times
25 April 1998

12

Why Fillies Are Politically Incorrect

The gender difference has always fascinated me, as it fascinates most of us. It has always fascinated me in horses, ever since I acquired a mad, gorgeous, hormonally challenged mare. I learnt that it was her nature to extort forgiveness: she did daft things, and would get upset if punished for them. So I tried forgiving her instead: and she liked that.

I bred a foal from her, a stroppy male, and to begin with, I was as soft with him as I was with her. It didn't work. I had to be significantly tougher: not physically rough, just stronger in mind.

This is a small, as it were, domestic problem. The question of how a top trainer handles the gender difference at the highest level of the horsey game had always intrigued me. So I went to an expert.

Let us surf into the weekend on a raft of wild sexist generalisations. Are males twice as good as females? Are males 150 times more important than females? Do you treat the two sexes just the same, like the two impostors? Or, on the contrary, do you treat them like two different species? Males from Mars, females from Venus?

I have always been rather struck by the fact that males are different from females; rather like most other living things on the planet. The question of how different, and in what way different, is the cornerstone not just of human civilisation, but of all life.

On, then, into Guineas weekend. Today, we have the 2,000 Guineas, the first classic of the season, in which three-year-old colts – that is to say, adolescent boys – will race along the brutal Rowley Mile. And tomorrow, we have the 1,000 Guineas, in which fillies, that is to say, adolescent girls, will run along the same unforgiving stretch of turf.

This is not politically correct, is it? I mean, are males really twice as good as females? Amazing, really, that these ancient race titles have not been changed. Really, we should have two races, each called the 1,500 Guineas.

Human fashions come and go. In my youth, girls were called women and they dressed in dungarees, garments of a plumber's mate that paradoxically emphasised their wearer's femininity. Recently we had the Spice women who must be called girls, and who claimed that the way to female power lies through utter silliness; and is it the males or the females who are sillier?

But as these cultural changes pass by, horses carry on breeding and humans continue to breed and train them. And if fillies have carried on being fillies and colts have carried on being colts, the way of treating them has gone through quiet and subtle changes, at least in some places.

When Clive Brittain talks about when he was a lad, he means lad as in stable lad. He rose from the ranks (having started in 1949) to become assistant to Sir Noel Murless and then a top trainer in his own right. 'When I was a lad, if you treated anything softly, it was because you were a softy. Basically, if it didn't move, you kicked it. And that was just the staff.'

You tell a gelding, but you ask a mare. That is the one of the oldest sayings of horsemanship. If you get stroppy with a mare, she will go sulky and sour. But a gelding wants to be put in his place. That is to say, his place in the dominance hierarchy; and his human handlers are part of that world view.

This is not to recommend yelling and knocking horses about. But with a gelding, it sometimes pays to be just that little bit insensitive. But you must never get coarse with a mare. When I came home from a long trip, I used to find that my mare would not talk to me. Turned her back to me in her box, staring at the manger. Not so much sulking as deeply hurt.

A Flat-racing trainer is mostly dealing with very young horses, the males still entire, the females flighty and virginal. But the principle of asking and telling holds good. Brittain is one of those trainers with a reputation for being 'good with fillies'.

It is a deserved one. He trained one of the best fillies that ever raced, Pebbles, who won the 1,000 Guineas in 1984, went on to become the first filly to win the Eclipse and the first British horse to win a Breeder's Cup race, the Mile, in the United States.

He also trained the 1993 winner of the 1,000 Guineas, Sayyedati. He has three contenders for tomorrow's race: Cloud Castle, Forum and Wenda. And he has brought them to race fitness by following the policy that you don't have to be a softy to treat a horse softly.

The military tradition is still a living part of horsemanship. There is a right and wrong way to do everything: men, animals and machines are all part of the greater machine. If you're not like everybody else, there is no room for you: man, horse, machine. Standardisation is the way armies work.

But a troop of racehorses is not a cavalry regiment; and trainers seek individual, not collective brilliance. One of the rituals of the racing stable is long and hard grooming: good for circulation and muscle tone, especially in the lad doing it. It is a ritual borrowed from military routine.

'I don't like to fuss a filly,' Brittain said. 'A filly often gets sour and fretful standing tied up and being dressed over. I like a filly to be with a lad' – a lad, of course, is often female these days – 'who can sense when a filly's in a bad mood, and stop brushing her, and take her for a swim, or a little walk and a pick of grass. That goes on all the time in my yard.'

Pebbles used to be impossible at morning exercise, always jumping about and spooking at nothing. Then Brittain realised that she was frustrated by the pace of things. The crowd of shambling, shuffling females all around her got on her nerves.

So Brittain paired her up with a very decent horse called Come On The Blues, a horse with a fine swinging walk. 'The two went off together, and did their exercise together. She went off behind Bluesy and never once put a foot wrong.'

Wenda would go up the gallops once, sweet as you like. But when she was asked to do it again, she would kick up a terrible fuss. Brittain changed her lad. Not a question of the quality of the previous lad: some horses and people click, and some do not. Ursula White took her over, and there has been no repeat of the once-only stuff.

Forum had a bad experience when she went to the races for the first time. She is a very nervous filly who panicked at the stresses of the big day. Brittain allowed her to recover by sending her back to the stud where she was born. She spent some time there grazing with the yearling fillies, peaceful, boss of her small herd. She came back much made up, and significantly tougher.

Cloud Castle has also had special treatment. 'Very light-framed, and she doesn't need a lot of work to get fit. In fact, she's only done one piece of serious work since she last raced.'

But it is the colts that will steal most of the headlines over Guineas weekend, especially if Xaar, the present Horse of the Century, hacks up as expected. In a sense it is right this is so. The simple facts of biology are the reason: a stallion can cover up to 150 mares in a year; a mare can have but a single foal, and is likely to have barren years.

But it is a genetic fact that every broodmare contributes as much to every foal as the sire: precisely 50 per cent. And raising a filly to greatness is perhaps the most ticklish task in racing. Moral: treat a filly like a colt, and you will make trouble for yourself. I will cease my sexist generalisation right there. Only adding that behind a successful filly, or a successful mare, you tend to find a person who is better at giving than taking.

Postscript: Cape Verdi won the 1,000 Guineas (see page 76); King of Kings won the 2,000 Guineas.

The Times
2 May 1998

13

No One Likes Us, We Don't Care

This piece was an attempt at writing a manifesto for horsey people: and also in the hope that it might change a few hearts and minds. I don't suppose it did. Horsey people receive a great deal of hostility; an irrational, atavistic loathing seems to invade the pleasantest and most civilised people when confronted with anything horsey.

Next week the British Horse Society (BHS) moves into its now annual and always quixotic attempt to tell the world that we horsey types really are quite nice people on the whole: in other words, it is National Riding Week.

There are no end of stunts. Photo opportunity at an equestrian centre in the East End. Angela Rippon taking her BHS riding and road safety test in Hyde Park. Visits to rescued ponies. Encouragement to would-be riders to give it a go. Attempts to get journalists to sit on a horse. The BHS continues its perennial campaigns for such things as safety, welfare of horses, access to the countryside, bringing horses to inner-city children.

Perhaps a few hearts and minds will be changed by National Riding Week, but really, this is an attempt to demolish an Everest of hostility with a hammer and chisel: chipping away at a great national prejudice. The Princess Royal, the incoming president of the BHS, says that there is an image problem. She should know.

Lest we forget, she was by a mile the least popular of the Royals. The reason for that was her intense horsiness: her determination to take her place as an elite competitor in the ultimate horsey sport of three-day eventing. She did so, becoming European champion, but most people prefer to remember the pictures of her falling off.

Spoilt, arrogant, horsey. Three synonyms, in public perception. When the Princess exhibited a similar go-for-it spirit in her presidency of the Save the Children Fund after retiring as an elite competitor, her popularity soared into the stratosphere. Improve your image: abandon horses. Diana, Princess of Wales, no fool at image-mongering, never went near a horse.

'Groups of people can be seen as threatening,' the Princess Royal told *Horse & Hound*. 'And people on horseback are not immune from this.' Or to put it another way: we are horsey, we are horsey. No one likes us – and, as a matter of fact, we are really rather upset about it.

Killer stat: 24.4 per cent of horse-riders earn less than £10,000 a year. This doesn't stop horses being extremely expensive and it doesn't stop a lot of very rich people from owning horses. But every form of living with money is about deciding on your priorities; and for an awful lot of people, horses are number 1.

Just because you feed horses on rolled-up £5 notes, and they go through shoes at a rate that would make Imelda Marcos blush, doesn't make horsey people rich. In fact, it makes quite a lot of horsey people poor. But that's our choice: no one asks for pity.

Just a touch less hostility. Do we sound a bit pathetic? But it is what we ask. Not simply because we feel unloved. Anyone who rides a horse on the roads has potentially lethal encounters on an almost daily basis. I do not exaggerate.

Killer stat: every day, there are at least eight road accidents involving horses and vehicles. One third of the 3,200 accidents that occur every year in what is, by definition, a dangerous sport are related to vehicles.

Too often, it is the car driver's hostility to horse-riders that makes accidents happen. Too close, too fast, too impatient, too irritated. And saying so can only provoke a bad reaction: shouldn't be on the bloody road in the first place. Arrogant, snooty, spoilt, privileged people who think they own the bloody road.

If wishes were horses, beggars would ride: this is a thought that has gone very deep into the British psyche. Remember Olivier's *Henry V*? The best bit was the chaps leaping out of trees to drag the snooty, spoilt, privileged, arrogant French off their horses.

The hunt saboteurs are not so much pro-fox as anti-horse, and I speak as a non-hunter. Sabbing is a re-enactment of Wat Tyler and the Peasants' Revolt, Jack Cade seeking to hang the mounted aristocrats. Aristocrats? Horse-riders, in truth, are a heaving mob; 2.6 million people ride every year, and more than two million of them are regular riders.

There are 565,000 horses in this country, 88 per cent of them in private hands – that is to say, not in racing yards or riding schools. That is to say, mugs like me. The equine industry is bigger, financially, than forestry, horticulture and fish farming – on a level with the British record industry, of all things.

Horse-owners and riders spend £900 million a year; checking through the bank statements I realise that it can't after all just be me. There are 6.3 million former riders and 2.2 million more who have never ridden, but really rather want to. This is a big industry, a big participant sport. And I happen to think it is a Very Good Thing.

The fact is that, in the main, horses do the very opposite of spoiling people. They teach children about caring. Adults too, for that matter. They teach you about the responsibilities of love as well as the rewards. They teach you about the pains and the disappointments of love, and they teach you about the consolations of love.

They teach you about the need for forgiveness and about the need to be forgiven. They teach you that a great deal of a relationship is slogging hard work. They teach you the difference between affection and commitment.

Above all, horses teach about privilege. For we are a privileged lot all right, we horsey people. But the privilege is not quite the way outsiders think of it.

Oh, I know we look dreadful, sitting up there, holding ourselves so tall and so arrogant, but riding with a straight back is how we are all taught, not to look good, but to stay in balance. It does look dreadful, the seated equivalent of the goose-step. And we are always looking down at people, so obviously we look snooty, even if it is not our own noses we are looking down.

We just look as if we are privileged: every bit of body language, our own bodies and those of our mounts, speaks or screams of privilege. And it is all absolutely true. We really are uniquely – all two million and more of us – privileged beings.

My horsey life has been a tale of endless privilege, from the first horse I really got on with, Ben Wyvis, a mad butty little

Australian thoroughbred, through to the dodgy and dangerous beast I ride today.

I have been privileged to spend much time in the border country between our own species of animal and this other species, privileged to live with animals whose ways are remote from us, but who, for some unfathomable reason, have a stange affinity for us.

No, really. Horsey people are just like most other people in the country. We have the same love of horses in common, do we not?

The Times
16 May 1998

14

Sheikh Mo (Part One)

This was a meeting I never expected to happen: sheikhs are too far above the rest of us to be bothered by journos. But in fact, Sheikh Mohammed and his Godolphin team were unexpectedly open, understanding that they have a public role in racing, which, like all professional sports, belongs to the public and can only happen because of the public.

You don't expect to have much in common with a sheikh. It is not the sort of thing that crosses your mind. But I had, oddly enough, forgotten about horses. You can't fake an interest in horses, you can't hide a passion. My delight in the lovely filly Cape Verdi set the ball rolling.

From there, our rather free-wheeling conversation spiralled off to other animals: we found we shared a passion for wildlife, for wilderness, for Africa. So far, so intriguing. But as we talked, the scale of Sheikh Mohammed's ambition became clearer. He is a man of blazing passions: and you can't help warming to him. The *Times* piece is followed by a piece on the Godolphin legend for *The Spectator*.

MORNING ON THE GALLOPS

Passion. No lesser term will do. Burning with it. Six in the morning, Newmarket Heath still deserted, first lot barely ready to leave the town's endless yards – and here was a man consumed with passion. Fretting quite dreadfully, for not even a sheikh can control the weather. Perhaps that is the attraction. Stay dry. Stay dry until Saturday tea-time. Then you can rain all you like. Let it not rain until the Derby is run.

I always love these glorious, fretful moments: the days before the race, when every horse is still a champion and anticipation freshens and fills in the morning dew. 'So do I,' Sheikh Mohammed said. 'This time is the best.'

There they came, the Godolphin string, all alike with blue silks on their skull-caps, lobbing along in a quiet canter. Sheikh Mohammed's binocular-bearer – is that his sole job? I wonder – handed the sheikh his bins. Quiet, intense, burning.

'She comes.' And come she did. Cape Verdi, the greatest filly that ever drew breath. Perhaps. We will know more at tea-time today. A beautiful, economical canter, skimming the turf with her daisy-cutting stride. Can you purr anxiously? If so, that is what Sheikh Mohammed was doing.

'I am pleased, yes. A good filly. But I don't want rain. If it does not rain, the horse with most speed will win. If it rains, the race will go to the most enduring. I don't want rain.'

Cape Verdi runs in the Derby. This is wild and wacky stuff, because she is a filly. The fillies have their own Epsom classic, the Oaks, which was run yesterday. 'We have won the Oaks many times' – as if a classic were a mere bauble, a bagatelle, a nugacity. Perhaps it is, but only for Sheikh Mohammed.

In theory, the Derby is a race for colts and fillies. In practice, only the boys contest it. The last filly to win the Derby was Fifinella in 1916. It is reckoned to be too much to take on the boys, especially as there is a classic for the girls alone.

'But this is the Derby,' Sheikh Mohammed said. 'The top, the top, the top.' The Oaks looked like a lay-down for Cape Verdi: after all, they are still treating the scorch marks that she left on the Rowley Mile after she claimed her blazing victory in the first fillies' classic of the season, the 1,000 Guineas.

But, startlingly, Sheikh Mohammed refused to play safe. He didn't want just one more classic. He wanted a Derby. His Derby. Perhaps every trainer in the land would have advised against this. It would, in a sense, have been every trainer's duty to advise against it.

But this is Godolphin. This is the Sheikh's baby, his pride, his joy, his passion. The horses are trained in the name of Saeed bin Suroor; there is also a racing manager, Simon Crisford. 'We all advise, we all have a vote,' Crisford said, 'but Sheikh Mohammed has two votes. At least.'

Sheikh Mohammed, listening to this, nodded agreement. He is a democrat: he always listens carefully to others before doing exactly what he wants. Which, in this case and in many cases before, is to defy conventional wisdom and go for broke.

'The public want to see the best horses racing against the best horses and I want to see it. Because – it is FUN!' It is hard to say the word 'fun' with such ferocity.

Sheikh Mohammed's wealth is dazzling, so much so that it obscures what lies behind it. Which is passion. Blazing, driving passion. Passion not for self-aggrandisement, or renown or glittering prizes: passion for horses. 'For all animals. I love to be with animals. If you come to my house, you see many animals – lions, tigers, gazelles.' No guinea pigs, then.

His earliest memory is being on a horse, his father riding behind him, and he aged two. His boyhood was spent with hard-running Arab horses, his youth race-riding. It is conventional to think of the racing sheikhs as languid playboys, another million-quid horse, another toy, another point won or lost in the private game they play among themselves.

Sheikh Mohammed is about as languid as a hurricane. Stand on the gallops with most trainers alongside most owners and learn one of the crucial aspects of the trainer's art: how, without offence, to explain to the owner exactly which horse is his.

This is easy for Sheikh Mohammed in one sense. There are 45 horses trained for Godolphin at Moulton Paddock Stables and they are all his, but he knows every one of them, forwards and backwards and sideways. 'I know more than a trainer,' he said.

'Trainers would not listen to me. That is why I started Godolphin.' His basic notion was, like all great ideas, simplicity itself. And audacious. The Godolphin horses do as wild horses do: they migrate south for the winter. They go to Dubai. The theory – no, the reality – is that they start the season a beat ahead of their rivals and the trick is to keep them that way.

Sheikh Mohammed has many horses in training all over the world and they are his delight; but he also has Godolphin and that is his pride and joy. 'I come here when these birds come,' he said, indicating the house martins wheeling and nest-building beneath the eaves.

Horsemanship is also his pride. He rides in endurance races: 100 miles is a long way for horse and rider both. He told a story about being overtaken by Crisford with a handful of miles to go. 'But I knew. I knew to save my horse. You feel his heart, through your legs, and you know what he has to give. So I saved him and, in a few miles, I passed Simon and his horse again. Both were finished.'

But which was the horse of a lifetime? No. That would be to look back. 'I have fine memories, I am grateful,' he said, 'but I look always to the next horse, the next great horse. Always to move forward. If you idle, if you stand still – you lose, you go backwards.' He waved his hands and tossed in lightly the perfect throwaway line. 'It is the same with running a country.' Sheikh Mohammed is defence minister of the United Arab Emirates, but he doesn't believe in sticking remorselessly to the day job.

'To train an animal. To find that it is the best,' he said. 'It is the same with a falcon. When you have the best, when you have trained the best.' Sheikhs like falcons, perhaps for their shared falconine profiles.

And the same fierce joys. There is drive to outdo and, when you have outdone everybody else, a desire to outdo yourself. I mentioned Ayrton Senna, who was a man of almost mystical passion, possessed by an unquenchable urge to beat his own achievements, again and again. Sheikh Mohammed nodded. 'I too am like that.'

We think of the racing sheikhs as rich dilettantes, boys with toys of incalculable value. Sheikh Mohammed thinks of himself as an elite sportsman, like Senna, not so much a driver as a driven man. Certainly, he has thrown money at his horses, countless millions of the stuff. So much so that we have failed to see what else he has thrown at his horses. His heart. His soul. Oh, and his brain, too.

With millions and no ability, he would have succeeded as an ordinary owner to some degree. Without the millions and with the same nature, the same horsemanship, he would probably also have succeeded to some degree. The two together – that is a powerful combination. Too much for most people. 'The top,' he said. 'The top, the top, the top.'

Postscript: Cape Verdi was never a factor in the Derby, unable to express herself in the traditional hurly-burly of the race.

The Times
6 June 1998

THE GODOLPHIN LEGEND

'The function of sport is the creation of legend. Discuss.' That is the latest essay in my undergraduate course, 'Sport and the Meaning of Life'. I suspect, however, that Sheikh Mohammed Al Maktoum would send in a very short answer. 'Yes', for example, or, 'What else?' Or, if in verbose mood, 'I know, I am that legend.'

His love of racing is, well, legendary. And at the heart of his multimillion-barrel sporting empire/dynasty, we have his operation called Godolphin. The name is a legend in the sport of legends. This weekend, two horses will contest the fifth and final classic of the year, the St Leger, carrying the colours of Godolphin.

Who is Godolphin? There was a Lord Godolphin, who owned the Gogmagog stables in Newmarket, but never mind him. The lord is peripherally famous; the real story is the horse, the Godolphin Arabian. Brace yourself for a legend.

There are three stallions who founded the dynasty of the

thoroughbred, from whom all racehorses are descended in the male line. The Godolphin Arabian was one of these. He was foaled in 1742, and was discovered pulling a cart (a water-cart, if you want the more precise version of the legend) in Paris.

He went to Gogmagog to serve as a teaser to a prized stallion called Hobgoblin. It is a teaser's job to investigate, then excite, the amorous propensities of a mare without getting any of the fun, preparing the way for one greater. But the legend tells us that the Godolphin Arabian fought Hobgoblin for the rights to a mare called Roxana. The Godolphin Arabian prevailed, and the result was a colt called Lath, and then, with a second mating to the same mare, another called Cade. They both went on to cover many a mare between them: a polyphiloprogenitive bunch.

The Godolphin Arabian carried on doing what stallions do best until he was 29. It was this admixture of Arab speed with traditional English stock that gave us the thoroughbreds that race today. There is a Stubbs picture of the Godolphin Arabian; it is not actually done from life, which is a rare thing with Stubbs, but it was a horse that demanded exceptions.

He has both the crest – high neck muscle – and the expression of a stallion used to deference, from mares, from humans, from lesser stallions. At his hooves, a Stubbsian cat regards him with an expression of undisguised mistrust.

The question of why Sheikh Mohammed chose to group together the horses closest to his heart under the name of Godolphin need not detain us long. The sheikh does not see himself as an interloper in the sport of English gentlemen: he is an Arab of Arabia coming to claim his own. He is a man utterly in thrall to the horse, to the legends, to the reality, and Godolphin is his joy and his pride. Stand with him on the gallops at Newmarket, watch the Godolphin horses blazing past, always tracked by the blazing eyes of the sheikh.

His is not a comfortable presence, any more than any other half-possessed legend-makers of modern sport. He is a man of burning intensity; one who knows he has made sporting history. History we make at once, legends take a while longer.

The Spectator
12 September 1998

15

A Gallop with a Racing Dynasty

This is another of those lovely horsey ladies. I had always enjoyed Clare Balding's company: we had, oddly enough, served on a couple of committees together, and when we bumped into each other at different sporting events, I often managed to persuade her to take a drink. She was no stranger.

We spoke on the telephone before Royal Ascot, and she agreed to do a piece with me. Perhaps, she suggested, I would like to come and watch her at work, when she was filming. I said it would be far more fun to ride a couple of horses. No interview: just ride a horse, and talk.

The top deck of a horse is, possibly, the nicest place in the world for a chat, and it can be revealing, too: riding horses together is far more intimate than sitting over a hot tape-recorder.

There I was, on a lovely horse on a lovely morning in lovely countryside with a lovely lady on a lovely horse beside me. Honestly, the things I am prepared to undergo to research this column are almost beyond comprehension.

The lovely place was Watership Down and to prove it, a squadron of rabbits burst from the top of the rise like the warriors in *Zulu*. The lovely horses in question were a racehorse called Pay Homage, and the trainer's hack, the not inaptly named Quirk, ridden by the hack who pens these words.

Journalistic innovation: perhaps the best way to understand a trainer is to ride his hack. That is to say, the horse he chooses to ride when he observes his string of a morning. Quirk is one of those horses who needs to impose his personality, an independent spirit who throws a pretty decent buck to express his solidarity with the horses galloping past. He is not above dumping his trainer on the grass.

Or perhaps the best way to understand the trainer is to chat up his daughter. The daughter was watching the string go by with an assessing eye, since I had usurped the hack for the morning. So it was her job to report back: this one worked like a train, that one had no steering and damn near ran down daughter and hack-riding hack.

Duty done, how about a little canter ourselves? And Clare Balding, for it was she, daughter of Ian, the royal trainer, who nudged Pay Homage into a . . . canter? Pay Homage was not especially in the mood for a canter and nor was the jockey. Balding is not a creature of restraints and half-measures. When in doubt, kick on: suitable motto for the horsey life and most other kinds.

Quirk set after the fleeing pair with a great deal of vim, giving away only about fifteen years, his jockey rather more. Watership Down: the soft countryside falling away with incredible steepness beyond.

And Balding – no, really, I can't call her Balding; next time we meet in the Badminton press tent or at a racecourse I would have to say: 'Hallo, Balding, would you care for a drink?' Clare is a star. Absolutely the latest thing.

Increasingly, television dictates the public perception of a sport. And Clare is racing. Next week, for the first time, she presents Royal Ascot as the central figure on the screen, the biggest challenge thus far of a brief media career that has already jumped prodigious heights. The jockey is not exactly overfaced, but hardly satisfied. 'All right, yes,' she said, responding to a piece of journalistic bragging on my part, 'but at least it was because of something you did. I want people to do the same sort of thing for me, because of what I've done – not because of who my father is.'

There is something terribly driven about Clare. She must please her father, she must do something so good that her father will have to shut up for ever. She wants to delight him and defy him at the same time. 'I thought I'd done that when I became head girl at school. Then I thought I'd done it when I became champion amateur jockey. Then I thought I'd done it when I became president of the Cambridge Union,' she said.

Instead, her father asked why she hadn't got a first, only a rather decent 2:1. Not exactly bullying, in the tennis-parent sense of the term, just a man driven by goals and the need to achieve. That is how he gets his kick out of life so, naturally, he wants to share it.

It is ever the problem of the children of conspicuously successful parents. Do you seek eminence in the same field? Do you rebel and become a nun or a drug addict? Clare took the third way: she sought excellence in another field entirely.

Andrew, her younger brother, is the one who will train: he is working with Lynda Ramsden and will move in as his father's partner at Park House stables, Kingsclere, in 2000.*

One wonders just how seamless a transition this will be, though Balding – Ian, that is – vows that his long-term retirement plan is to lose a bit of weight so he can ride point-to-point. When in doubt, etc.

Which is all of a piece with a phenomenally restless man who has run the yard since he was 25 and, at nearly 60, is a classic portrait-in-the-attic job. Baldings are built to last. He trained Mill Reef: enough said. Mill Reef was one of the Horses of the Century who really was one of the Horses of the Century. He trained Border Arrow to be third in the Derby; before that he was third in the 2,000 Guineas.

This is not, then, a household of modest expectations. I first met Clare when we both sat on the working party of the British Show Jumping Association. She was then doing only radio, but was already making waves, and not just in racing. She covered, and still covers, all sports. 'How come you played so badly?' she has found herself asking. Asking, in fact, the questions that listeners, rather than sports stars, want to hear. Clare rather specialises in doing the sort of thing that's Not Quite Done.

She is forceful and effective in committee, full of original ideas of the very good and the very bad kind, and bursting with missionary enthusiasm for the horsey sports. We should share them more. Knock down the old nonsense about class and privilege. Enjoy the beasts.

We met again as fellow judges of the Martin Wills Memorial

* In fact, this happened a year earlier, when the Ramsdens gave up training.

Prize, a competition for young horse-writers, and we formed a powerful – certainly very loud – alliance, one based on the above principle. Never mind Sport for All: we stand for Horses for All. Clare took to television presentation much as you would expect from one of her quite extraordinary self-confidence. 'You're nodding too much,' her father said, by way of celebrating her elevation. After the retirement of Julian Wilson, Clare got the job as the face of BBC racing.

Her first act was to slag off the BBC's racing coverage as 'complacent and arrogant'. There was, and still is, an endearing trait of loose cannonism in her. She is filled with ambition, but not at the cost of becoming someone else.

Clare, like Quirk, and like Quirk's usual rider, is not without quirks. She will impose her character on proceedings. Her father's tough, critical nature has given her the drive to achieve without denting her self-confidence. She refers to her 'rather frightening' CV; her self-confidence is equally alarming. And she is but 27.

Just after she got the BBC job, she was asked to ride in a celebrity race. Shall I? she asked her agent. If you must, the agent said. But for God's sake, don't fall off. With news of the appointment just out, it would make a picture story right across the national press. She didn't fall off. She and Pay Homage won the damn thing. She staked her reputation in a business built on reputation at the turning point of her career. A wise person would have ducked out.

But Clare is not wise, not in the what's-in-it-for-me kind of way. The race was, well . . . irresistible. And so we asked our beasts for one last canter back across Watership Down, bunnies diving for cover as we went. Irresistible. When in doubt, kick on.

The Times
13 June 1998

16

The Ride of a Lifetime

This is one of my favourite pieces ever. I rang up my old friend and teacher, Debi Thomas, and asked if I could ride her dressage horse. This was an act of some cheek. Amazingly, she agreed to it, and thus gave me one of the most memorable mornings of my life.

We have heard a lot, as the World Cup rumbles endlessly onward, about the jogo bonito, the beautiful game, but let us turn our attentions to the most beautiful game of them all, in comparison with which all other games are ugly, sordid and graceless.

It is a beautiful game, but it is not about beauty. It is about power. Dressage looks effortless, for rider and horse both. Well, you should have seen me when I got off one of the country's more classy dressage animals this week. Physically shattered, having used every muscle I possessed, and a stone or so lighter as well, looking as if I had emerged from a shower of boiling water. And positively radiant with self-conceit.

Look, this is going to be a modest piece, full of self-deprecation, showing a becoming – and really rather touching – low opinion of my own capabilities as a rider. But please understand right now that, behind the irony and jokes, stands a horseman of truly awe-inspiring ability.

Well, that is certainly how I felt when I leapt nimbly – and then collapsed – from the back of the glorious Truday after an hour and a half of work at the most advanced moves in dressage. Walter Swinburn said after winning the Derby in 1981: 'I was just a passenger on a very good horse.' I am in a position to know exactly what Swinburn was talking about – and I bet I felt just as good as Swinburn did when Shergar exploded away from the rest of the field.

Debi Thomas allowed me to ride Truday because she knows what an amazingly good rider I am. Or if I am not amazingly good, it is entirely her fault. She was my teacher for four years, when I lived near London and kept my horses at the livery yard that she runs in the grounds of the stunning Wrotham Park.

Thomas has schooled and competed Truday up to the level just below the Grand Brix, which is the highest level of all. There are only a handful of Grand Prix competitions in this country in a year, which gives an idea of how rarefied the business is. Truday will be making her Grand Prix debut next season, or perhaps the one after. She is 12; one of the many beauties of dressage is the glorious slowness with which talent expands and develops. Of rider and horse both.

Back in the yard, behind the Palladian mansion, stands Coronet. I have watched Thomas start and school this horse from nothing.

The horse has had her on the floor more times than she cares to count. The stable girl was carrying a bandaged arm thanks to Coronet. Thomas fractured her pelvis in her best fall from Coronet so far.

Please understand, then, that dressage is not a game for wimps. Why persist with such a difficult animal? Because of the talent. Not submissive obedience, for Coronet had none of that, and anyway, dressage is nothing to do with submission. It is, as I say, about power. What Coronet has is glorious athleticism, seething promise, extravagant movement. Channelling the talent, that is the challenge. Finding the harmony. Getting a tune out of the horse, in the dressage riders' expressive phrase.

Dressage is at the heart of all good riding. If you can ride well, you can do dressage. I expect Frankie Dettori could ride a decent dressage test with half an hour's practice; I expect half the stable lads in the racing industry could do the same, if they gave their hearts and minds to the task.

At Hickstead on 7 and 8 July, they are running what they call the Eventers' Challenge, in which the eventers and the show-jumpers take each other on in an event involving show-jumps, cross-country fences and – to sort out the men from the boys – a four-star dressage test. That is to say, the highest level of all, by eventing standards. Not so very high by my standards.

No, I take that back, obviously. What I mean is, not so very high by the standards of the dressage specialists, people such as Thomas and Truday, but it will be fascinating to see how show-jumpers such as Michael Whitaker and Roderigo Pessoa tackle the dressage. But that is enough about them. Let's have some more about me. I adore dressage, which naturally means having to defend it.

People tell me it is 'unnatural' and they tell me it is all about the rider's power over the poor horse. But horses don't do unnatural movements. They can't. Every single movement a horse performs in a dressage test is one he will perform when he is turned out in the field.

It is the horse's power that matters, not the rider's. In dressage, you are balanced on a knife edge. The more power you ask for, the more delicate the balance. To my inexpressible joy, I managed to get Truday to perform the transition from passage to piaffe: the horse a coiled spring beneath me as she performed the single most physically taxing move in dressage. The rider asks for forward power and blocks it off at the same time; forward movement is converted into the most extraordinary gravity-defying spring.

Trying to repeat this scintillating moment, I was just a fraction coarse in the way I put my request to the horse and, rightly resenting this, she shot upwards like a rocket from a milk bottle: full vertical rear with added dynamic spring from the back legs. It takes a horse of rare power and athleticism to do that. If you think dressage is the soft option, think again.

Horses canter with one foreleg leading the other and they can change this in a single stride. This is called a flying change. It is one of the acid tests of a good horse and I managed to bring it off. Under Thomas's instruction and following my request, I soon had Truday changing leg every fourth stride. And every third stride. And every other stride. And then, gloriously, quite impossibly, every single stride. I was no longer riding. I was dancing. Truday was dancing. I had been transported, willing passenger, into the highest reaches of horsemanship.

I was allowed to get closer to the heart of dressage than is normally permitted to any save the very best. It was a quite extraordinary privilege. It was not just the sense of driving Michael Schumacher's car, hitting a golf ball with Tiger Woods's driver, facing Allan Donald with Steve Waugh's bat. It was also as if I had borrowed a little of Schumacher's, of Woods's, of Waugh's ability – because the horse, schooled so superbly by Thomas, allowed me to take on just a fraction of her skills. For a strictly limited period of time, I had been loaned something of the abilities of the very best riders in the world. And, for a few scattered moments, as we passaged, as we piaffed, as we danced, I was one of them.

As I dismounted, offering these splendid ladies my very best thanks, Thomas said: 'I'm so glad you were able to get a tune out of her.' Some tune it was, too. Beethoven's Ninth, I reckon. Nothing less.

The Times
27 June 1998

17

A Spot of Mindless Violence

I thought I might put this piece on polo here, sandwiched between a piece on dressage and a piece on riding side-saddle. I put it here for the sense of balance it gives. I had a wonderful time, some years earlier, learning to ride polo style, and I might have thrown my life and my little all away in pursuit of this gorgeous game. But my inability to hit the ball enabled me to see sense: to find a sense of balance if you prefer. But God, it was fun.

This is the week in which I shall lay bare the secret of polo. It is. in fact. the best-kept secret in sport. You probably thought that polo was all about money, privilege, swaggering about in boots and cutting a swathe through the daughters of the English aristocracy. Of course that is all true, especially the bit about boots, but it is not a secret at all.

Now, as the ten-goal polo professionals of Argentina prepare to converge on the fat-cat patrons for the English polo season which begins next month, and the ponies begin to relearn the meaning of hard work, my mind goes back to a summer's afternoon when the secret of polo was revealed to me: *polo is the dirtiest game in the world.*

I was invited to learn the game and I took up the invitation with alacrity. A wonderful horseman called Nicky Williams taught me to ride polo style, all spinning and stopping on a dime, and it was bliss. Then I was invited to play a practice game. I was helped by one of my team-mates, Williams's son, Roddy, who was then in his early teens and a young lad of quiet confidence and exquisite manners. What a nice boy.

Alas, once the game began he turned into a ravening beast. With one bound, the air filled with 'fucks' and 'bastards'. I had thought this was a game for gentlemen: I learned that it was a game whose sole purpose was to bring out the cornered wolverine that lurks beneath the surface of every public-school man.

Miles out of my depth in the first chukka, I tried in vain to hit the ball. On the few occasions I got within easy commuting distance of the damn thing, I swung mightily and missed. It was hateful and I was in a fury. I changed ponies for the second chukka in a mood of uncontrolled embarrassment.

And thus I released the wolverine inside. With its help, I learned that polo is a mixture of dressage and Graeco-Roman wrestling. I rode in a frenzy. I rode with murder in my heart. I had, in short, joined the club. I ignored the petty distraction of the ball. I rode off opponents in a whirlwind of shoving shoulders, digging elbows and wounding words. I gave whacks and I received them, but I was too insane with competitiveness to feel them. And once – oh rapture! – I tipped some genius of a Latin off his pony. I can still recall the glorious sight of his headlong dive to the ground and the altogether unexpected knowledge of English he revealed in extremis.

That was the joy of it: the intoxication of combat. the voluptuous peril of duelling at the gallop. I resolved then and there to become a full-time polo player the instant I became a millionaire. I have played much football and I know about whacks. But football is a game for gentlemen. If you want to play dirty, play polo – especially with a polite young English lad.

Now I learn that Roddy Williams is a major talent in the game. He is part of the Young England team, a team of English-born five-goalers. none older than 21. They are a breath of fresh air. The traditional polo team requires two one-goal professionals, normally from Argentina, one one-goal patron. who needs to stay on his pony and pay the bills, plus A.N. Other English one-goaler. Young England has four five-goal lads. They need a sponsor, so if you have £25,000 they would love to meet you.

Polo is a frequently used marketing device. Marketing men see sunlit lawns. elegance, lots of nice drinks, young chaps in lovely boots and a pleasing atmosphere of getting quietly smashed in the midst of unending jeunes filles en fleur. But they haven't got a clue. The most suitable product to represent the true spirit of polo is a custom-made sawn-off pump-action shot-gun. A great game. I really must be a millionaire in my next incarnation.

The Spectator
23 March 1997

18

Riding Side-saddle

Some of the stories I have most enjoyed have come in the form of dares. Side-saddle riding is one of the more obscure parts of the horsey world, but it has its fanatics. And one of these dared me to come down and try it for myself.

What red-blooded man could resist such a challenge?

There are some writers whose greatest pride is the absolute sure-fire, knock-you-dead quality of their opening sentence, or paragraph. So, in deference to the – journalistically, rather dated – cult of the intro, I offer you a choice.

a) There is an old joke in which a Frenchman and an Englishman see a woman pass by on a horse. 'What a beautiful woman,' says the Frenchman. 'What a beautiful horse,' says the Englishman. For once, I felt the European and the Englishman within me unite in perfect harmony.

b) I have done some surreal things in my time, but the afternoon I spent riding side-saddle with the King's Troop, Royal Horse Artillery, was something of a collector's item.

I was invited up to Pittern Hill Stables in Warwickshire by the Side Saddle Association, and more or less the first thing I set eyes on was Clarissa Dawson, the side-saddle rider of the year last year, mounted on a rather splendid grey, manifestly side-saddle and in full slap and drag.

It is one of the facts of life and of mythology that women and horses go well together. The horsey life is filled with women: the highest achievers, the most ordinary everyday leisure riders. I have heard the opinion expressed that there is something not quite right about horsey ladies. Au contraire, I assure you.

There is an endearing craziness about side-saddle people. What's the point of it all? None, really, but if you start looking for a point in everything you do, you are going to lead a very impoverished life. There is no point in horses, if you take that attitude. A car will get you there so much quicker.

In every walk of life, you meet the nutcase who pushes things just a little bit too far. You find rifle-shooters who don't believe that the ammunition-makers know their job and that they can only be properly served by ammunition they make themselves. In bird-watching, you meet people with the most fantastic optical equipment. Sometimes they are very good at recognising birds. Side-saddle riding is a bit like these extreme types. It is absurd, yes, but what the hell's wrong with that? It is also beautiful, and that is enough to be going on with.

Now I bet you thought that side-saddle was an instrument of oppression, an archaic implement based on an outmoded modesty.

Bringing back side-saddle is like bringing back the chastity belt. But if you thought in those terms, you could not be more wrong. Before the invention of the side-saddle, women simply sat on horses sideways. Hard to stay on, almost impossible to control your horse. You needed someone else to lead.

The side-saddle offered not repression but freedom. It gave women not further chains, but real control. In a proper side-saddle you can gallop and jump, and if the horse should throw a few bucks and the odd stand, you are probably in a better position to deal with the problem than a rider astride.

Demure it ain't. It's rather dashing. But you have got to be rather in love with the gear, with the tack and the clothes both. It is not everybody's cup of tea, but the horsey world offers more different sorts of cups of tea than any other branch of sport. There are few things more lovely than perfect turn-out – provided that someone else has done the brushing and the plaiting of the mane. Full side-saddle turn-out is dramatic. But you must know how to ride. A perfect riding position is vital.

Dawson rides tall in the saddle, shoulders well back. There is nothing remotely modest about a woman riding a horse, even if she is wearing riding habit, top hat, Edwardian cutaway riding jacket, waistcoat, high stock and, of course, veil. It is to-die-for gear, and if you want sure-fire, knock-you-dead impact, this is the horse sport for you. 'The really difficult thing is to drink a gin and tonic through the veil,' Dawson said. 'The only answer is to sink all pride and use a straw.' I felt better for learning this.

And no, I was not joking about the King's Troop boys. There were three of them: the former master saddler, the present incumbent, and his heir apparent. Saddlers are a different kind of nut. They, too, are gear maniacs. The construction and fitting of the saddle is to them an unending source of fascination. So it should be. Saddlery is both crucial and appallingly difficult, and it takes a certain mind-set to grasp the task. Obsession is merely the starting point. Which is why the boys were here.

The Troop used to have a female vet, who, on ceremonial occasions, was required to ride side-saddle. Fascinated by the challenge, by an entire new range of saddlery, by a complete new set of gear, the saddlers were agog to learn more.

First point: a side-saddle is not at all insecure. Side-saddle riders, schooling a crazed youngster, have been known to wish that they had a decent chance to fall off. Second point: the position is not unnatural and twisted. You keep your shoulders and hips in line with the horse, just as you do when riding astride. It is rather like sitting with your right ankle on your knee: not modest, but easy and natural.

The two posts on the saddle, one for each leg, hold you in place. Riding is not about clever positions, it is about understanding the mind and the movements of your horse. If you can ride one way, you can ride another.

It had its day, side-saddle riding. I was shown an ancient point-to-point side-saddle; with it, no longer was it rude for a lady to point-to-point. But, after the war, side-saddles were consigned to attics across the country. Riding astride was no longer considered arriviste and unladylike, and the art was, if not lost, certainly mislaid.

But the revival was inevitable. Just as at Bisley, you find nutcases with black-powder weapons, and on the road you find other nuts with perfectly tuned Bugattis, so the side-saddle revival had to come. The Side Saddle Association was formed in 1974 and goes from strength to strength.

It is both gorgeous and crazy. It is just one other way of enjoying horses, and I don't have any problem with that. 'You did really well,' Dawson said. 'Have you done much side-saddle riding before?' Well, really, of all the left-handed compliments I've ever been given . . .

The Times
18 July 1998

19

A Day at Pony Club Camp

One of the great regrets of my life is that I was never a member of the Pony Club. Oh, of course I regret it for all the right reasons, many of which are to be found below. But just think: at senior camp, you might be the only 16-year-old male among 50 or 60 females.

I was dared to do this story by my friend Rose Hart, who has been deeply involved in the Pony Club for years. It made a perfect contrast/complement to my outing, a few days earlier, to Ascot for the King George. It's all about horses, you see.

This week, it is this column's proud boast to have penetrated the most hated organisation in the country. Not the British Fascists or the InterCity Firm or the Hell's Angels or the Masons: no, I have set my sights much higher.

Cunningly disguised in a flat cap and stout boots, I moved among the members without attracting attention, listening to the secrets, playing a double role, prepared always to pass these secrets on. And it worked. I have got to the heart of the organisation that attracts more fear and loathing than any other.

Yes, I have penetrated the Pony Club. To be precise, the Waveney Harriers Pony Club camp (junior section). There I passed unrecognised among 60 ponies, 59 small girls and one small boy, and a raft of instructors and volunteers.

You will admire my courage, I know, because this does, indeed, sound like a truly frightening prospect. But I was up to it. Soon I found myself at the bareback jumping class, taking on the essential task of catching ponies and helping girls with wobbly lower lips back onto their ponies.

Actually, the first time I did, it was near disaster. I am more used to legging people up onto racehorses. The first fallen girl I gallantly assisted nearly got thrown clean over the top of her little pony. She saved herself with a frantic grab at the mane and myself. I apologised, promised to get the range right next time.

Terribly brave, all these little girls. Bareback jumping makes falls inevitable, some of them outright comic, with the faller giggling when picked up, and some of them quite nasty. Plenty of tears. 'Deep breaths now.' And then back on again and take the jump again too. 'Hurray, hurray! Well done, Anne!'

And it is all innocent and hilarious and touching, but I know that the hackles of my readers are rising. And so I must go on and tell you that the Pony Club children are not all the daughters of the snooty well-to-do, and they are not all spoilt brats with gobfuls of silver spoons.

And of course, you won't believe me, but I must at least go through the motions. Walk through the car park, where the parental cars were all parked (parents do a lot of helping, it's that kind of organisation). And yes, there were plenty of shiny new four-wheel drives, many of which will never go off road.

But there were also many ancient vehicles held together by such things as rust and habit, and some of the rust looked pretty weary. All right, you say, but it costs a lot of money to buy a pony, so cars or no cars, all the parents must be rich and therefore all the kids spoilt. All 60 of them.

But in a community, especially a rural one, horses have a way of circling around. Ponies are beloved and often very long-livers. So they are outgrown and passed on: as gifts, as long loans. There were some ponies in their twenties, who had done a dozen or more Pony Club camps, some of them with half a dozen or more different partners.

Tack and riding clothes also go round and round. You can keep a pony on do-it-yourself livery (that is to say, you do all the work) for as little as £10 a week. Which is not nothing: but life is all about priorities, and for some families, the pony is the thing you make your sacrifices for.

Pony Club camp is an annual summer holiday tradition: five days of endless instruction and riding and competition and caring for the beast. It costs £90 for five days, including all the food for rider and pony. It works out at less than a quid an hour. How does that compare with Disneyland Paris?

There were, indeed, some well-off kids with their own rather expensive ponies, and some of them, but by no means all, were rather good at riding them. There were the tenner-a-week kids with their beloved hand-me-down veterans, some of whom were absolute mustard. And there were also a lot of children on borrowed ponies: a horse of their own for a whole five days and, in many cases, for the first time.

Four in this situation had never in their lives ridden outside a single small oblong of sand in the middle of Norwich. Hacking out into the country, and then, gloriously, charging round a cross-country course – oh, brave new world that has such horses in it.

Observe the children at the start of the cross-country course: preparing for the mad scurry beneath the massive ancient oaks of Sotterley Park, over a series of hard, unforgiving obstacles. Terror is a poor word for what some of these children feel. Observe the faces before their turn comes up: don't bother with the blindfold and the last cigarette, let's just get it over and done with.

Observe the watermelon grins afterwards, the self-delight, the discovery of undreamt-of courage, the gratitude to the merry beast beneath who had given them such joy. This is not a small lesson to learn.

And there are plenty of other lessons, too. The pony is looked after by the child. For many, this is the first time they have ever had so much responsibility – for anything. Naturally, everything they do is checked, but they have to do it and get it right. It is a way of learning the responsibilities of love: a way of learning that love is not a straightforward business, and one that you do not ever get on your own terms.

Pony Club camp is, all in all, a long lesson about the nature of love. Love requires courage, it requires responsibility, it requires strength, it requires forgiveness. Horses teach you these things; and in the five days of the camp, these large matters are ineluctable.

The Pony Club has recently become a charity, which gives it serious responsibilities far beyond the entertainment of privileged children. It is also the largest youth movement in the country after the scouts; it has 120,000 members in 15 countries. And it is changing, from the ancient traditions of elitism to an organisation committed to the notion of Horses for All.

Horses are, for some people who care for them, a vector for learning – learning about life, about love, about other skills. Horses are for some a phase in the growing-up process. For others, they become part of a way of life. For rich or poor, horses become one of life's priorities.

By one of those odd coincidences, the dreaded mobile phone rang out from my pocket at I walked past the bending poles towards the field where they were judging tack and turn-out. ('And did you do all the plaits yourself?') It was a message from Sheikh Mohammed, in response to something I had written about the victory of his excellent horse, Swain, in the King George at Ascot the other week, one of the richest races in Europe. Part of the message was that the reason he seemed less than effervescent in victory was because he had the previous day taken part in a 100-mile endurance race.

Just another person who loves horses not wisely but too well. And there I was in the middle of a muddy field surrounded by 60 more of them. As a result of my infiltration, I can report the secret at the heart of the Pony Club. It is joy.

The Times
8 August 1998

20

Peta Beckett (Part One)

You will perhaps know how the story of Peta Beckett ended: she was killed by a fall from Watermark in 1999, one of five event riders killed in that terrible year. I have included this piece, not out of a desire to be depressing, but because Peta was, simply, wonderful.

Lovely to look at, delightful to be with, a gorgeous rider in every sense: I had a lovely morning, talking about horses, or to put it another way, life. I want to celebrate her absolutely splendid liveliness; for hers was a life worth celebrating.

Some people reach the summit in a single mighty bound. Others seem to be carried to the top, as if the top were the only right and proper place. Still others crawl every step of the way on their hands and knees. The method is immaterial; the point is the summit.

And for all of them, but perhaps especially for the last category, the final pitch is the hard part. At the highest level of every sport, the actual ability of all the contenders is very close to being equal – and yet there are serial champions and there are perennial top-20 types.

The final pitch is the hardest because it is a mental leap. And most of the contenders for the top places know this. Dominance hierarchy: it is not necessarily the biggest or the strongest horse that is the boss in the field. It is the one who believes in his heart that he is number 1.

And so to a chunk of deeply undulating countryside near Banbury to meet a couple ready – or perhaps not ready – to make that small step, that quantum leap from jolly good to top-class. The horse, Watermark, was so laid back that he started dozing in front of the camera.

The rider, Peta Beckett, a three-day eventer, faces perhaps the crucial few days of her life over the weekend at the Doubleprint British Horse Trials Championship at Gatcombe. Her CV contains the added exoticism of experience as a catwalk model. Actually, she hated it and went back to the horsey life without a backward glance, but it is a nice line. And she certainly doesn't doze in front of the camera.

The air around her crackles. I often speak to people as they bustle about the yard – horsey people are good bustlers – but not with Beckett. It was not that she was too fast in the straights: she out-turned me, like a polo pony, darting here and there, grabbing this, grabbing that, going back for this. 'Butterfly brain,' she said of herself, with a truly excellent smile.

Lashings of charm and welcome of course. She is perhaps a calm person at heart, but certainly not a still one. 'I'm terribly impatient,' she explained impatiently. Adding: 'Except with horses.'

This is one of the many mysteries of the horsey life. Horses bring qualities from humans that are not expressed elsewhere in their lives. Rough-edged people find that horses bring out untapped reserves of gentleness; the hard-nosed find sentimentality; self-doubters find certainty. And sometimes, the meek find the most relentless form of driving ambition.

Naturally, the air crackles around Beckett, because, at 32, she is at the point when her career could break the sound barrier. The final pitch – the one about mental strength, the one about her rightful place in the dominance hierarchy of her sport – stretches up before her.

She has been patient as well as drivingly ambitious: but she has now reached the point with her number 1 horse at which only the latter quality will do. It has been a stunning achievement to get as far as she has. But that single step farther is what she will be judged on; what she will judge herself on.

The ultimate revelation of naffness comes from those people who choose 'My Way' on *Desert Island Discs*. There is consolation as well as defiance in the song's central claim. Anyone who has trained a young horse can empathise with it: trying to do it well, trying to do it right. That is true, no matter what level of achievement you aim for or reach. I feel it myself with the young hooligan that I ride.

Beckett rides tall, a lithe five foot eleven inches. Watermark, or George, or even Lardy for his slug-a-bed ways, came to her as an insurance write-off. His first job with her was to have two and a half years off work. Then work could begin. And she tried above all to do it right. To take on an insurance write-off with two and a half years' rest is a bit of a gamble. To put in the years of time involved in bringing him on is a colossal investment. Why? 'Something about him. Just something about him.' Another of the eternal mysteries of the horsey life: the horse has something the rider believes in, responds to.

And sometimes, gloriously, vice versa. Patience. No short cuts. No schooling gadgets, no draw-reins. Beckett had the belief that her hands, her patience, her entire horsey self were good enough to do the job the slow way. The careful way. 'It's the difference between having a slave and having a partner.'

Nicely put. Eventers ask more than riders in other disciplines and to those that ask in the right way can sometimes be given.

Beckett has been given a fair amount already. Watermark/George/ Lardy has completed six three-day events and never been out of the top ten. Goal: the World Equestrian Games this autumn, to compete as an individual. For this she needs a good Gatcombe, a good run in the final selection trials at Henbury Hall at the end of the month.

It is with Watermark that her hopes lie. Slouching out of his box like – well, like a horse, really. An ordinary sort. Then Beckett is on top and working: and a different animal. Looks a full hand taller – 'you should see him in competition' – and moving with easy balance, relaxed self-confidence. Beckett put him through some exquisitely neat flying changes, and a big flashy extended trot.

They were working in a field with a camber like the roof of a house, but that was no problem to Watermark. The loose horses milled about, but fell back at a glare, an infinitesimal laying back of the ears. Dominance hierarchy.

And it was all highly promising, but there comes a time in life when you have to give up being promising. You've either done it, or you haven't. That realisation tends to come at – more or less – the age of 32. The realisation that there is plenty of time and that it is running out. That you are at your own peak, or thereabouts. And if you are a peak-orientated person, you must summon up your own peaking powers to reach the summit of your choice.

'Butterfly brain,' she said again, striding in and out and in and out, in her splendidly eccentric riding clothes of half-chaps and sling-backs. And later: 'If I had brains I'd be dangerous.' Stock dismissives. Pay them no mind.

She knows what a good job she has done with Watermark: to take a horse from write-off to within touching distance of the top. Training an event horse is long-term business, and patience is one of the great allies as well as the great virtues, and it must by definition take years, and it always involves the overcoming of more setbacks than you would believe possible, but there comes a time when only one sort of time actually matters. That is to say, now. The smile is to die for: the air crackles.

The Times
15 August 1998

21

The Pig-cart Horse

When a very smart PR person rang me up and sketched out the details of this story, I crowed in delight: it is a perfect tale, an absolutely impossible pony-book adventure. And every line of it true.

So I went to Hickstead to meet Mumu and his charming and handsome (the photographer, Gill Allen, spent an awful lot of time photographing him) rider Carlos Ribas. It was one of those occasions that has the journo in you rubbing his hands in glee. And the horse even more stunning than his rider.

This story is so charming, so delightful, so utterly absurd that I am not quite sure where to start. It is about a little horse that used to pull a pig-food cart in the slums of Rio de Janeiro and is now a crackerjack international show-jumper.

The horse – he is just about big enough to be called a horse, rather than a pony – has the absurd name of Mumu. And if you saw him today, tied up outside a gypsy encampment, you would not turn a hair. Mumu would fit right in.

The story of how he went from the pig-cart to the International Arena at Hickstead – he is scheduled to jump in the Speed Derby this afternoon – is full of absurd twists and turns. To be frank, I don't expect anyone to believe a word of it. I hardly believe it myself and I spent most of one day this week in his company.

In fact, his rider, Carlos Ribas of Brazil – 'that horse is my life' – left me in sole command of the horse while he went and walked the course that he was about to jump on his second- and third-string animals. I walked Mumu in his head-collar, giving him a good pick of grass, leaning my right elbow on his back, which seemed to come at just about the right height.

Mumu, unfazed by me or by anything else that has happened to him in his life, ate grass as if there would be none left in the world after twelve o'clock and tolerated my elbow in good part. There is an air of effortless decency about him. It takes rather more qualities than that to get to his position in international sport – but he just doesn't show them.

I was conscious of people swivelling towards us. What's this funny-looking little coloured horse doing here in the elite stabling? Surely that bloke should take him down to the ring with the kids' ponies.

Later, watching Ribas ride Mumu down to the practice arena, I was again witness of the horse's head-turning qualities. Not as in, my God, what a wonderful animal. But as in, what the bloody hell is that doing here?

Daddy, I want that one. Every parent of a horsey child knows that experience, but the little girl in Rio wanted the jolly, little, coloured horse that she saw pulling the pig-cart. Being a little girl of strong will – little girls who fall in love with ponies tend to have strong wills – she had her way.

'They bought him for . . . a piece of banana,' Ribas said, flipping his fingers to show the incomprehensibly minute nature of the sum. And so Mumu became a riding horse and continued until the little girl, now a bigger girl, decided that she wanted something with a bit more scope.

Ribas said that twinkling at the ironies – but he had yet to come into the story at this point. The horse was sold on, going to a riding establishment in São Paulo, and his new owner started to jump him. Education intervened: his owner went to university, asking the riding school boss to do some work on her horse when she was away, a regular request in the horsey life.

This he did – and found that the more he asked the little horse to jump, the more the little horse jumped. 'He asked me to help him buy it,' Ribas said. 'To go halves. And I say no. And again and again he ask me. Again and again I say no. But, in the end, I say yes. To . . . make him quiet, yes?'

But, as a shutting-up ploy, it failed. The friend kept suggesting that Ribas actually ride him. And Ribas kept refusing. Ribas likes to cut a handsome figure on a handsome horse: he admits that his vanity blinded him to any qualities that the horse might have.

Basically, he was not going to be seen dead on top of a ridiculous, coloured horse that was about half the size of a decent show-jumper. Most show-jumpers are built big: 17 hands, a great deal of muscle and – as you would expect from great athletes – they swagger about like Linford Christie.

But, above all, there was the fact that Mumu is a coloured horse. This is a generic term, covering all kinds of animals – palaminos, duns, strawberry roans – but what you normally understand from the term is an animal with two colours, the sort you see outside gypsy encampments.

Piebalds and skewbalds: Mumu is a skewbald, chestnut and white, colours scattered at random about a slight frame. There is a tendency for people to be snobby about coloured horses, even more so outside England. In Brazil, such horses pull carts, or at best walk about with tourists on their backs.

So Mumu was not the horse to ride if you were seeking to look good, to establish your credentials as a serious contender in the sport of showjumping. But then came the Brazilian national championships and Ribas found that all his horses had gone lame: fickle luck of the horsey life.

Fickle good luck, as it turned out. 'Ride Mumu.' 'No.' 'I tell you, ride Mumu.' 'No.' But there was no other horse to ride. So Ribas took him into competition – and won the top class on each of three successive days.

So the new partnership was catapulted into international sport. Ribas's father bought the other half of Mumu, not for a piece of banana. Ribas and Mumu are now based in Belgium, where they ply their trade in the big-money shows of Europe. And Mumu rises to each challenge as he rises to each jump.

'Where does the power come from?' I asked. For Mumu is not even a big 15 hands. He had a high wither or shoulder joint; measurements are taken from the ground to the wither. A fraction less bone in the shoulder and Mumu would be categorised as a pony.

And he is not stocky, he does not have an eye-filling back-end, the place from which the power comes. He just is: a slight, utterly unprepossessing horse with odd markings and huge ears that are pointed at the tips like Mr Spock's. Where does the power come from?

'From his heart,' Ribas said. 'He does not feel small to ride.

And he is a fighter.' He is that all right. He made his Hickstead debut on Thursday and won, against some notably hot competition, the Hickstead Salver. A still greater challenge lies ahead today. 'I don't mean he fights me, he never fights me. He wants to fight the challenge, he wants to achieve for me.'

A rare and wonderful feeling. Some of us have even met it, just once or twice, at our much lower levels of the horsey game. At any level, any level at all, to have beneath you a horse who will, it seems, go through fire for you – that is rare.

The Speed Derby today is a very big step for Ribas, inexperienced at 24, and for Mumu, still short on experience at 11. 'If he finds trouble, I shall stop him, retire from the competition. I don't want to spoil him, to upset him, to hurt him. He has time, we both have time. We can maybe come back next year.'

And he repeated: 'You have to understand. The horse is my life.' And, of course, I understand. I understand about love, I understand about the rare and precious thing that Mumu has. I know about the horse that would go through fire for you and I know what it is to feel that you would as willingly go through fire for the sake of the horse.

I know the thing about a horse that is absolutely priceless, priceless beyond all possible computation of valuation. Even when the horse itself cost a piece of banana.

Postscript: Mumu jumped well in the Speed Derby, but stumbled badly when ascending the notorious Derby Bank, an obstacle he had never seen before. After that, Ribas nursed him home to an honourable completion.

The Times
22 August 1998

22

Supervising My String on Newmarket Heath

Jeremy Noseda is an old friend of mine: I have always enjoyed it when our paths cross. From the very first, he talked a good deal about when (not if) he would be training in Newmarket.

And so it was natural to pay a visit to his new yard, his new house, his long-in-gestation hopes. Most yards that you visit in the way of business tend to be old and successful, with a routine of success. With a new yard, all the routines are new, the expectations high and constantly changing. Jeremy is filled with confidence: and apprehension. A fifty-fifty mixture adds up to realism, if you can get it right.

His first season, in fact, turned out to be very good and solid; in fact, highly respectable for a first-season trainer. But he wanted something better . . . he always does.

Scene: a beech grove near the Limekiln gallops. Newmarket, where else? A gorgeous little spot, calm and secluded, the horses winding down from their gallop, lowered heads, lads holding the reins by the buckle.

A rider on the trainer's hack surveying the string, nodding approval of the horses, of the long calm after the brief frenzy on the glorious, brutal open spaces of the galloping ground – and also the butt of the trainer's words. The trainer was on foot, I was riding the hack. The hospitable Jeremy Noseda had legged me up onto Boris, the better to savour his string in action – but then Noseda and I go way back.

'That feeling,' he said. 'Out here on the gallops. You say, I know that horse is going to win the Derby. Win the King George. Win the Arc. You know it has to win, you know it can't lose.' We had not seen such a horse that morning, though there are some nice horses there all right. 'That feeling, there's nothing to touch it, nothing,' (anticipation being a more reliable drug than fulfilment) 'but when you have won, that moment, if you could put it in a bottle . . .' If you could put it in a bottle, you'd spend your life in the gutter with the bottle at your lips, but the real thing doesn't come in bottles.

There are few enough who have known that rapturous kiss of total fulfilment in this game, but Noseda has. Which is something of an oddity for a trainer in his first season.

Not many first-season trainers have won the Derby, the King George and the Arc all in the same year. And no, of course it was not this year, we haven't had the Arc yet for a start. It happened in 1995, the horse in question being Lammtarra.

I use the term 'he' loosely, far more loosely than Noseda would himself. He was, after all, part of a team. 'A great team, a great time.' Lammtarra and the other huge winners of the year were all part of

Sheikh Mohammed's Godolphin operation. The person who held the trainer's licence was – is – Saeed bin Suroor. The person who held the purse strings and made the final decisions was – is – Sheikh Mohammed.

For a civil servant, the great reward is in being indispensable, in being appreciated by Those Who Really Know. But for some, that is not enough. 'It sounds stupid, but I wanted not just to win races, but to win under my name. Under my name. Do you understand?'

I patted Boris, an eight-year-old graduate of the Galway Blazers. 'None better,' I said. 'Damned if I want someone else's name on the cover of my novels.'

And so we have Jeremy Noseda, trainer of racehorses. With 40 horses in training, including a group winner – that is to say, the winner of a pretty decent race. 'Does it sound arrogant if I say I am glad to have got that one out of the way?'

Well, it doesn't sound too humble. I might enjoy a humble racehorse trainer, but I wouldn't send him a horse. Arrogance, though, is something you tend to find when there is a lack of other qualities to back it up, a kind of bluster. There is no bluster about Noseda.

But then he learnt his trade under the superlative John Dunlop. That's where Noseda and I met, when I spent a year with Dunlop researching a book, back in 1986. A racing yard is full of foot-soldiers, indispensable NCOs and various wet-behind-the-ears subalterns called pupil assistants.

Noseda, conspicuously dry-eared, was promoted from pupil to full assistant. 'Watch him,' Dunlop said. 'I think he might be rather good.' Since Dunlop uses the same tone of guarded understatement when he talks of Derby winners, I watched Noseda.

From Dunlop to number 2 at John Gosden's in Newmarket.

Talent-spotted, taken on by Godolphin. Triumph and then the parting of the ways when anonymity became too great a burden for Noseda to bear. Then nearly two years in Los Angeles, training at Hollywood Park, but with his heart crying out for England. For Newmarket: the big skies and the endless gallops, the air crackling with promise.

There's money in the background as well as talent – a good combination. And now he can take the credit and the blame. 'Had my first last the other day.' The horse picked up an injury. Not his fault, but his responsibility. That's training. And no sheikh, no expensive horse to follow expensive horse.

So building a string is the priority: 'Can't go without the horse, my lord,' as the jockey famously said. You don't win horse races without horsepower. Noseda is in thrall to the magic, a debunker of mystique. He aims to give his owners the fullest information of any trainer in racing.

With 40 horses, there is no need yet to delegate, so there he is with dirty hands, wearing a storeroom coat of the kind that makes you look, in the immemorial words of one of Dunlop's stable lads, 'like a pox-doctor's clerk'. Bandaging horses' legs himself, rugging them up.

A small detail. You should have seen the hay. I want to write passionately about hay, even though you will laugh at me . . . but take my word for it: it is the most beautiful hay you could ever see and probably the most expensive; Noseda buys it from the United States. 'My horses must have the best.' Rockets need rocket fuel.

'And here's a nice sort . . .' Brief litany of the breeding, the blood is blue enough, but a shade paler than he has been used to. '. . . This is a big, backward two-year-old, should come to himself next season.'

I laughed. 'How many big, backward two-year-olds have you

got?' 'Enough.' 'And I suppose they're all going to come to themselves next season?' 'That's the plan.' Promise: the air of Newmarket is something you can dine on, promise-crammed.

The string left the beech grove, the trainer, in his ridiculously flashy motor, headed back to the yard, the horses following, me and Boris among them.

Noseda will have been in business as Noseda for a year come November. The foundations have been laid. A good team around him, some decent horses, owners ready to back promise of horse and trainer both – a double gamble, but a pretty sound one.

Perhaps the best preparation for life as a trainer is a horse like Lammtarra. Because then he knows about it all, knows the feeling of the kiss of victory, the taste of the finest wine of all. And he wants another taste so badly that I think it must rather hurt.

The Times
29 August 1998

23

Carl Hester: a Brush with Perfection

Dressage is the loveliest of all the horsey disciplines, and I have always enjoyed my attempts to bring it to an audience beyond its devoted followers. When in doubt, go for the best: never a bad rule in journalism. No journalist is ever frightened by the obvious: and Carl Hester was the obvious person to go and visit.

It was another of those mornings of watching a talent too extreme for envy, still less emulation. It was a deep pleasure; and as I have said many times, I do try and find stories entirely for my own pleasure.

You can't dance in a half-nelson. Conclusion I came to after an entrancing morning with a man with the hands of an angel and the drawl of a chorus boy, and a bunch of horses who clearly believe that gravity is for wimps.

The national dressage championships are held at Stoneleigh this weekend, and Carl Hester, stung by his unexpected exclusion from the British team that goes to the World Equestrian Games in Rome next month, is expected to carry all before him.

Carl Hester is the perfect who-he? superstar. Just about everybody who reads this column will wonder who he is: but a few who follow the rare discipline of dressage will groan. Not him again. How many more months is he going to be flavour of the month?

I heard a rather good story about Hester, about the esteem in which he is held, and about dressage, about every one of the subjectively judged sports. A dressage event: Hester rides into the arena in all his usual finery, halts, salutes the judges. Horse stands on its hind legs, a fit of totally unacceptable behaviour. A sneering voice in the audience: 'I reckon that's worth 12.'

Explanation: in dressage, each movement is marked out of ten. Reason for joke: Hester is so much the flavour of this and every month that whatever he does, the blind, entranced and loving judges will grant him ridiculously high marks. Is there anywhere in sport as bitchy a world as dressage?

Well, journalism, for starters, but that's by the by. All subjectively marked sports are fraught with tensions. Such and such a woman wins because of her mascara and pearl earrings; such and such a man wins because of the way he works his epicene charm with the lady judges. And on and on.

Dressage is about beauty, and something beautiful is always lost when you mark it out of ten. That is the contradiction in all the judged sports, especially skating and gymnastics. Contenders inevitably seek the highest possible level of achievement: naturally they want not only to be beautiful but to be adjudged the best.

Hester may have the hands of an angel, but he also has the competitive drive of a human.

But then all of dressage is about contradiction: that is the beauty of it. It is about the horse's glorious freedom of movement: but the freedom is to be expressed at the request of the rider. I am reminded, if I may say so without giving offence, of the prayer with the lovely line about 'Whose service is perfect freedom'. Something of the beautiful paradox of dressage can be found in that line.

A glorious morning, watching Hester ride horse after horse after horse. Always first riding them in a strange fashion, in direct contradiction of my own early riding lessons: 'Shorten your reins up, Simon, you are not hanging out the washing.'

But Hester rode with reins like washing lines, sometimes making adjustments with his hands more or less round his ears, in strange communion with the horse beneath.

And then the middle period of the session, when the horse, instead of warming up in the long, low, flowing and forward lines, was asked to work in a different outline, a different shape. Power on: this is the period in which gravity is defied. 'You must save on your shoeing bills with this one,' I said. 'Doesn't bother touching the ground.' Half a ton and more of horse, floating like the will-o'-the-wisp.

British dressage used to be a contradiction in terms. That is changing fast. It is booming at every level of achievement, including the highest. The entire understanding of the sport has changed: dressage is far more an aspect of freedom than of repression.

'Expressive paces.' A standard piece of dressage jargon that. Sounds daft, I know, but don't scoff. Movement is how a horse expresses himself: he has his being in movement, expresses his mood, meaning and purpose in body language.

It is the partnership aspect of it all that is crucial: each partner's understanding of the other; each partner's generosity towards the other. If understanding and especially if generosity is a one-way street, there is a consequent loss in beauty. That is what all dance is about. And it is that quality of generosity that Hester has in overplus. How do you separate a rider's physical skills from his temperament? How do you separate the acquired physical skills from the innate ones; his acquired mental posture from his natural character?

You can't, obviously. But watching Hester ride is to be struck by generosity. He has the priceless ability to make a horse acquire a skill without fuss. Watching him teaching a horse to make the movement with the lovely name of flying changes, he was quite unfazed when the horse made an error, almost non-judgemental. He praised with quiet pleasure when the horse got it right. It's easy. It's no big deal.

Actually it isn't easy, it's bloody hard for rider and horse both. But this generous, unflustered approach struck a perfect balance: horse eager to please, untroubled by fear of getting it wrong. It takes a lot of riding skill to be able to be that generous. Most riders are not good enough to train a horse without resorting to punishment, without, in the jargon, negative reinforcement. It takes a generous nature: it also takes a riding position of phenomenal balance, depth and control. That level of skill is something most horse people can watch without envy: it is beyond our abilities if not beyond our understanding. I'd love to be that generous myself. I have the mind to do it: but not the physical skill. Nor am I unique in that.

On the ground, Hester is easy company, charming, witty, full of camp jokes. The horses dry off after their hosing down 'under the hair-dryer'. And so on. Hester was a natural, coming to horses late in life, on a whim to be a jockey, for the sole reason that he was, at 16, a small lad.

He went into horses, grew and grew and so did his talent. First as an eventer, then as a pure dressage rider. And the best teacher, too, I was told by one of his pupil assistants. Sympathy, understanding, communication: many people good with horses are good teachers. Progressive training is what it is all about.

Communication. There has been so much guff talked about the ghastly movie, *The Horse Whisperer*, that most horse people will now throw up at the suggestion that there is a kind of magic some people have and others don't.

We are all of us horse whisperers; that is to say, we all seek to communicate with horses, and to do right by them. Hester is no magician. He does exactly the same things as the rest of us. Only better. Because of that immense skill, that immense sympathy, he can be what he is – generous to a virtue.

The Times
19 September 1998

24

Dressage for the Blind

I have done some frightening things on horses in my time, but this beat the lot. I have met some pretty courageous people who ride horses, but they are all – we are all – cowards when we stand next to this lot. But bravery is pretty good stuff: you don't walk away from brave people feeling pity, or terror. You walk away feeling, in an odd way, exhilarated. This was a truly great day. I felt dizzy with the shock of it all for some days afterwards. It was a day that went pretty deep.

Writing my speech on a long and winding railway journey. No, I really can't say that, it's in really rather poor taste. On the other hand, they sound a pretty resilient lot to me. So when the time came, I stood before them invisible and said it anyway.

'Ladies and gentlemen, this is not the first time I have taken part in a dressage event for the blind. But on previous occasions, it was the riders who were sighted, and the judges who were blind.' There was an audible intake of breath at this, a tiny pause in which I thought, oh dear, I've gone too far this time. And then the most gratifying shout of laughter. A blind person who rides horses is going to have to be pretty bloody tough, after all.

I know. I have done it myself. I did it, but I had one of life's built-in get-out clauses. I could take my blindfold off any time I wanted. Slightly important difference, that.

I had been invited to an event called Bridge 98, at Pittern Hill Stables in Warwickshire. Last time I had been there, I had been feasting my eyes on a lovely lady riding side-saddle on a lovely horse. The sort that, as we horsey people say, really fills the eye.

This time, I was at an event that brought together a couple of dozen blind riders from all over the country; the oldest was aged 85. The idea was to go through a basic dressage test, watched by a proper dressage judge who does a good deal of work for Riding for the Disabled (RDA).

The blind riders wanted to stage this, their first championship, separate from the excellent RDA, because the problems of doing a dressage test without looking where you are going are quite different from the usual problems of RDA riders.

A dressage test is a series of manoeuvres in a small arena. These can be very easy, or very difficult. The test I learnt for the occasion was so easy I could have done it with my eyes closed. Just a figure of speech, that. As you will see.

You navigate around a dressage arena by letters: each point is marked by a letter, always the same letter. The journey BXE is the same journey in every dressage arena in the world. And you ride much of any test by looking at the letter you are aiming for: that glance lines your body up with the direction of your intentions, and that is how direction is communicated to the horse.

The problems of riding blind dressage begin to become apparent. The answer is talking letters: tape-recorders around the arena, each chanting a monotonous message: 'A . . . A . . . A . . .' And a brave woman standing in the middle of the school saying: 'X . . . X . . . X . . .' Aim straight at her.

'In a way, jumping is easier,' Tim Gebbels, who was organising rather than competing this time, said. 'Oh, jumping's much better than boring old dressage,' Sarah Craig said. Well, everywhere you go in riding, you find people saying this. I just hadn't expected it here. I'm naive, that's my trouble. 'I used to have a horse I galloped on the beach,' she said, 'and we jumped all the breakwaters.'

Well, as I was to say later in my bad-taste speech, I've always felt that the best way of clearing difficult obstacles is to do so with your eyes closed – but this sort of thing is really rather out of my class.

Sarah's test was good and, not entirely to my surprise, bold. You got the feeling that if she had to ride through the wall to complete a 20-metre circle, that there wall was going to have to go. But the winner was Julia Ponton, who fell off, though cleverly managed to do so before the test started.

The horse spooked sideways, and she was gone. That is the trouble with riding when you can't see the horse: you can't read intention movements. Always, by definition, you are a beat late, reacting rather than acting.

But reunited, unfazed, she rode with great style and confidence, no need for a sighted helper at her side. Then it was my turn. I got a splendid-looking old thing the colour of Frank Cooper's Oxford. Sad to know such a horse from touch alone, I thought as I climbed on board.

I rode for a few minutes, learnt a bit about the horse, and more about his attitude. Then it was game on. I was given one of those masks you wear in an aeroplane when you try to get some sleep. I put it on and changed the world from top to bottom.

The first surprise was that riding itself was not a problem. Horsey people often talk about feel: you can't teach it, they say. Well, I could feel whether my horse was tracking up, moving correctly, holding himself in a proper outline, when he was supple and cooperative, when he was resisting. That was the easy bit. The first problem was direction. I could not tell when the horse was turning. Hear the letter, look across blindly to where the next letter should be, ears on stalks. Have we turned? Or are we still heading for the wall?

But the real problem was information overload. The letters with their monotonous repeating messages: 'A . . . A . . . A . . .' The test: what the hell am I supposed to do next? The problems of groping for a spatial awareness I did not possess. The thousand complex messages from the horse. A computer, bombarded with too much information, will cease to function, and so did I.

I removed my mask for a sneak peek, a luxury unavailable to the real contestants. I was not where I thought – at least 30 metres out, and the arena was only 40 metres by 20. I was so disorientated I wanted to throw up.

Start again, sighted helper back at my side. 'Are we going to try the canter?' 'Damn right I am.' I got a proper response, too; thank you, Marmalade Horse. And somehow we got through, final salute to the judge mere yards from the right spot, walk out on a long rein, and rip the mask away: rejoin my own world. Sweating as if I had completed a cross-country course.

There are easier ways than this of having fun. But people don't always want easy things, blind or not. Is it all about challenge then? The north face of the Eiger, expanding your horizons, feeling Better as a Person? Is it all about those worthy things that disabled people are supposed to be so frightfully keen on? Personally, I think it is nothing of the kind. What matters is not Releasing Your Potential, but being with horses. Horses just happen to do the business for some people. And we will put up with all kinds of things for the privilege of being among horses. It is not a matter of blind people Exploring Their Limits: it is just horsey people doing their horsey thing. Which is what this column is about every week.

Sarah buttonholed me after I had handed out the prizes and the rosettes. 'And I want you to start campaigning for cross-country riding for the blind,' she said. There is a motto in the horsey life: when in doubt, kick on. But I did not need to explain that to the riders of Bridge 98.

The Times
10 October 1998

25

Betting: Barney Curley (and Me)

I used to enjoy betting at the races; I then discovered a far more efficient means of getting rid of money on horses. Racing is about betting, however, whether you choose to wager your own money or not. And the romance of the gamble is nearly as deep as the romance of the horse itself: both have something of a belief in magic; in something that is going to take you a little way beyond the ordinary.

Barney Curley is one of the great gamblers of our time, a bizarre conundrum of a man. I went to see him at his book launch. Most of the accounts in this book (the one you are reading, that is to say, not Curley's tale) are of splendid horsey chats: moments of intimacy when the guard drops around the stable yard. This did not happen with Curley; mainly because he never drops his guard, never has a cosy chat, seldom has anything in common with any other living human.

This piece is not an account of a pleasant meeting: it is about witnessing the performance of a legend. It is followed by a piece on my own life as a gambler, from *The Spectator*.

BARNEY CURLEY'S GREATEST GAMBLE

There was a time in my life when I used to see crocodiles every day. That was when I was in Zambia: thousands upon thousands of crocodile sightings. Once, only once, I saw a crocodile move quickly.

Or rather, I didn't see it move quickly. I saw it motionless in the water. A nanosecond later, I saw the antelope in its jaws. They are deeply impressive beasts, the big crocs. Crocodiles are supposed to be cruel and cold and vicious: but not so. They just move to a different rhythm from us mammals.

I had a similar feeling when I met Barney Curley, legendary trainer, legendary gambler, legendary legend. There was something oddly still about him, though it did not seem to be the stillness of inner calm. But something oddly impressive.

It was a merry social gathering for the launch of his book, a day of mingling and small talk. Curley was there as a fish or a croc out of water, lacking both small talk and practically all other assimilable qualities. As if he had arisen from the swamps to be present.

Nothing wrong about him, but it was simply clear, right from the start, that he moves to a different rhythm from the rest of us. Perfectly bald, a moustache that looks like an uncharacteristic lapse of attention when face and head were last shaved, and an air of utterly challenging self-possession.

And every few minutes, a controlled rant. It seems to be his preferred conversational technique. Shoulders back, head thrown back, hips well forward: good strong Northern Ireland vowels. The Jockey Club. The British Horseracing Board. The bookmakers – ha! The bookmakers, the so-called Big Three. The bookmakers' lackeys, the racing press.

And the racing press let it all wash over them, because you can say what you like about Curley and Curley can say what he likes about anything – and be assured that he always will – but he is that eternally forgivable thing, good copy. Legendary legends always are.

Curley is a gambler. He also trained for two years to be a Jesuit. He is Irish. So naturally, you expect a Chaucerian figure, a jolly tonsured friar and lovable reprobate, a scallywag, long on life force, not altogether to be trusted, but a thoroughly merry, profane and irreverent fellow.

This is about as far from Curley as it is possible to be. Curley is a spoilt priest all right, but spoilt priests are, more often than not, intensely religious men. If anything, he is somewhat stiff in his moral joints. In a sense, his entire life – gambling coups, confrontations with racing authorities, battles with bookmakers – have all been part of an urgent need to Do the Right Thing. His life seems to be driven by the urge to stand up and be counted. The opposite of a rebel without a cause: a man perpetually in search of a cause to fight for.

Gambling is thought of as a vice and a pleasure, and so a professional gambler, it follows, must be a man devoted entirely to pleasure. Not so, of course. That saurian coldness is what counts. A real gambler – betting for profit rather than amusement – must know when to strike and how to do so with speed and utter ruthlessness.

Curley's best story in the book is the Yellow Sam Coup, in which a horse trained by Curley was backed with every cent that Curley possessed – and still started at 20–1. He managed this extraordinary feat because the horse ran at Bellewstown, a small racetrack in Ireland, which then, in 1975, had only one public telephone box.

At the heart of the coup was Curley's ally, Benny, who occupied the phone box for a full half-hour, not putting the phone down till they came under starter's orders. That way, the on-course bookies would never hear about the fortune bet on Yellow Sam and so they would not shorten the odds. And it is the prices on the course that the off-course bookies must honour.

Constantly apologising to the people in the queue for the phone, Benny explained that a relative was dying in hospital – no, she's rallied, thank God – no, she's sinking, sinking fast – until the race was away and the fate of the bookies was sealed.

That all added up to something like £300,000: 'But I must confess, I've no real idea. I gave up counting.' All of which is part of racing's store of legends. But Curley seems untouched by it all: not specially interested in the horses – he has always delegated the day-to-day chores of training – or the money. 'I wouldn't have a clue how many winners I've had. I have always wanted to beat the system.'

A rather splendidly revealing remark. No matter what the system, Curley wants to be beat it. Selling your house is a nightmare for us all: Curley raffled his. He then went to train horses in England. Got into a row with the Jockey Club about the way a horse had been ridden. Got warned off. Then got his licence back – and bet with anybody who'd take a bet that he'd train ten winners in the couple of months before the year ended. Won his bet: yet another legend from the legendary legend.

It has been a rum life and one you never expected to see in print. A gambler, to be successful, has to be awfully fond of keeping his own counsel. Curley is not a warm, open, engaging man – not to strangers. There is a mystery about him; there always will be. A confessional such as this book cannot give more than a clue about the rhythm he lives by. 'I broke Nick's heart,' he said of Nick Townsend, his ghostwriter. 'He'd want me to speak of my life and tell my story. And I would always prefer to speak of things like life in the hereafter.'

Tough task for poor old Nick, then. 'Besides, horse racing doesn't matter. It doesn't matter in the least, it is totally trivial.' In the book, he says: 'I don't have that much interest in money. I think I'm capable of doing something better.' He then added words I thought never to read in a sporting autobiography: 'If I'm honest, I feel I have wasted my life. I've never felt comfortable in racing, or have achieved anything that really mattered.'

Maunderings of an old fellow – well, he is 58 – on the brink of retirement? Not a bit of it. Curley has now decided to take on yet another enemy. His new target is global poverty. Or to be more specific, the problems of Zambia. He has founded a charity called Direct Aid for Africa. Target: a million quid.

And, of course, that's why he agreed to do the book. To tell a strange tale of a man who moves to a different rhythm and to raise money for Africa. I did a biography of a rum cove myself once (born, by coincidence, in Zambia). I called it *A Singular Man*, which would have done all right for Curley. But he chose to call his *Giving a Little Back*.

The Times
17 October 1998

BARNES'S GREATEST GAMBLE

Just think of it, if I had bet £1, just a single, measly quid. Yes, Frankie's going well, so why not? Had I done so, I would now be jangling not £1 but £25,095 in my pocket. A heady thought, but then gambling is all about heady thoughts.

Frankie Dettori famously went through the card at Ascot on Saturday, riding seven successive winners. A £1 accumulator on Dettori's seven rides throughout that heady afternoon would have reaped the aforementioned sum in profit. 'Sometimes,' Dettori said. 'He is on your side.' God is a big character in racing.

Driving, as it happened, through the rain-spattered streets of Dublin the following day, the eternal taxi-driver told me how he had looked at the papers and decided that the time was ripe for a wager on the jockey of the moment. He had put money to the thought, with the trifling difference that he selected the mounts of Pat Eddery rather than Dettori. He had, however, risen above this misfortune: 'I'll not back that f—er again.'

Moments like this cannot fail to awake the punter that lurks within us all. Who could fail to respond to the glorious notion of £25,095 purchased with a single, golden coin? To buy not only money but a strike for the righteous against a wicked world, to become for £1, omnipotent.

It is hard to feel omnipotent when you work for the *Balham and Tooting News*, but I did, occasionally, manage it. For the office stood hard by the far from inaptly named Mecca bookmakers. I would intersperse the writing of reports on Tooting and Mitcham FC and the laying out of the parks' football league tables with perusal of the *Sporting Life* and, later in the day, with living it.

Turn towards Mecca with 77p to play with – yes, the 10p win patent, plus tax – into the world of fag butts and those special half-length ball-point pens that bookmakers so lavishly provide. You need never be at a loss for the means to write out a betting slip. And the wonderful, matter-of-fact voice of the Extel blower in the wall: 'Raining Lingfield . . . Plumpton they go down.' And then he would read a result, knowing, but not letting on, that there was heaven and hell in every line.

It has been suggested that people who imagine that racing is not about gambling must also imagine that dancing is not about sex. But gambling is also about sex, or so a psychotherapist friend assures me. 'It is about the fantasy of controlling the universe,' he said, 'as in, I am the special chosen one of God. But as soon as you talk about control, you are asking questions about the relationship with the parent of the opposite sex.'

'But gambling is mainly about losing,' I said. 'Precisely. The constant failure to win provides a container for your depression. It externalises it. It's like supporting a bad football team, or buying a lottery ticket every Saturday. It provides weekly but manageable proof that God doesn't love me. And the point of that is that losing is in fact a safer option than winning. Ask Oedipus.'

Ah, but the joy of it. I remember my pelting heart as I stood in Mecca, face turned towards the blower, awaiting the results of a photo-finish. They had said the name of my horse first – was that a good omen? Or, on the contrary, a very bad omen? And then the announcement, almost too wonderful to credit: Swing Alone – stupid name, and one I shall never forget – first, and Barnes was master of the universe, was monarch of all he surveyed, including that bastard of an editor.

But I no longer bet. I recall my last moment of equine omnipotence: the backing of a 42–1 shot which, in racing's aromatic jargon, pissed up. I invested my considerable winnings.

I acquired my first horse, to ride, not to race, an addiction more terrible and far more expensive. These days I no longer bet, I pay farrier's bills.

The Spectator
5 October 1998

26

The Greatest Show-jumper Ever

I have had some extraordinary days in the course of pursuing horsey stories, and I have met some extraordinary people. The adventure that follows was one of the most extraordinary of the lot. It was Lisa's sheer ability that got to me.

The idea was that we all went to Germany for the day to visit the yard of Paul Schockemoble and choose a horse for Lisa. Lisa Murphy is 23 and a crash-hot showjumper, competing this week in one of the big events at the Horse of the Year Show at Wembley.

My main job was to hold the horses' heads while Lisa was adjusting the stirrup leathers and to give her a leg-up when she wanted to get on. 'Most of the people I know sort of vanish when I need a leg-up,' she said, 'and when I do get someone, they're sort of ridiculously gentle. They're just frightened they're going to pull it off, you see. But it's tough, you can be pretty rough with it.'

We had already had the routine problem going through security. Lisa can empty her pockets of small change, but she still makes the metal-detector gate bleep. She told the security man matily: 'It's coz me leg's plastic.' And gave it a light thump for illustration. It rang like a drum.

How do you keep a horse straight? By holding it between your legs. How do you make a horse go forward? By using your legs. How do you stop a horse shifting sideways? By using your outside leg. How do you make a horse check its speed? By using your legs to move forward into the lesser pace. Impulsion – that is to say, power: crucial factor in the horsey sports. It comes from your legs.

Lisa was born without a chunk of left leg and an amputation took away a bit more. So there she was on horse number 1, a near-black Westphalian mare. They seemed to get on rather well, so we put the jumps up to something near five feet and Schockemohle suggested she follow the vertical with an oxer, a fence nearly as wide as it was tall.

You need power, precision, straightness and control. You simply cannot get over the fences without these things. Showjumping is a matter of cold nerve and finicky accuracy. It is all about the focusing of power.

Another horse, another leg-up. Once again, I managed not to pull the leg off. A muscly chestnut, a flaxen mane to match Lisa's. He hit the second element of the double with a loud crack. Schockemohle made an adjustment to suit the horse's bigger natural stride. And they flew.

Big, round, brave jumps: the horse and rider each combining boldness with finicky care. That's showjumping. No, that's very good showjumping indeed. And no, of course I didn't think what a brave girl and she with just the one leg. Naturally, inevitably, I thought: 'Well, what a wonderful bloody rider.' I thought: 'I wish I had balance like that, fluency like that.'

She doesn't come from a horsey family and, naturally, she was cherished. Naturally, her parents wished to protect her from the slings and arrows of the world. A friend had a pony and she wanted a go, but her parents thought: 'Lisa can't do that. Protect the child from disappointment.'

You might as well try to protect the wind from disappointment. Lisa does things. She had a go, liked it, wanted more. Talked her parents into getting her a pony, also took up ice skating. Today, she skis, plays squash, badminton. That's for fun; her ambition, her life, is horses.

Like all sports, showjumping is pyramid-shaped and always, there is a wide band of people just below the pointy bit at the top. Lisa is part of this band of young riders, fighting to climb that crucial level higher. They are all very, very good, all seeking to make that transition into excellence.

I couldn't go without the horse, my lord, as the jockey said, as I say just about every week. Sheikh Mohammed, the kids in the Pony Club games at Wembley this week, Lisa Murphy: they all know that you cannot do it without horsepower.

Lisa has a top-class horse called Hello One. Another very, very good horse would help, hence the trip to Germany. Her sponsor, QBE, wanted to get a horse for Lisa – another top-class animal. It is all about horsepower and there is nowhere better to go than the kingdom of Schockemohle in Lower Saxony.

So it was a day of crucial decisions; and all the while, Lisa's riding skills watched by Schockemohle, one of the great masters of the sport. Rather like showing your sixth-form poems to Ted Hughes.

Being a rider myself, there was no help for it. I was consumed with vulgar curiosity about the practicalities of riding, of jumping at this level when fortune has given you one leg fewer than the usual number. Lisa, you will have gathered, was never likely to be overwhelmed with embarrassment.

She rides deliberately crooked, that's the secret of it: very short on the real leg side, much longer on the plastic side. 'I need a horse that's a bit brave. I can't leg a horse over the fence if he wants to stop and have a good look.'

We talked about the practicalities of training a horse, of starting a horse from scratch, which is, in some ways, a good deal harder than riding a clear round on the finished product. Lisa has brought on a top-quality horse from nothing herself and that is something to be proud of, no matter what your tally of legs.

'You've got to work hard, it doesn't come easy, and it can be so frustrating. You know you have to leg a horse up on to the bridle and of course that's just what I can't do. I have to do it in a way that takes longer. It's hard for the horse as well, you see. They get confused.'

She acknowledges the help from her coach, John Popely, her fiancé, Ken Ashe, another young show-jumper hustling to get into the top part of the pyramid. You need help, you need the horse, but you need the ability, as well. The horse won't go without the jockey.

So what about the Paralympics? 'I couldn't do that. I couldn't. I don't consider myself disabled. I couldn't go in and take a medal off a real disabled person. I want to ride in the Olympic Games.'

A grey, called Petpur, finer in looks, a more complicated

character than the chestnut. I think it was the fifth or the sixth horse of the day – I was getting confused. And straight away he showed his ability and more challenging nature. When he got it right, he got it very right indeed. But we had a plane to catch, Lisa had a Wembley class to ride the following day. Handshakes, thanks, departure. We'll let you have a decision on Monday. The black Westphalian mare? The bounding chestnut with the flaxen mane? The complex grey? 'What do you think?' she asked me.

'Well, they're all the right horse. Each one has talent and it's a different sort of talent in each one. Each one needs a rider good enough to bring out the talent. And the good news is that whichever horse you pick is going to be ridden by a very talented rider.' Was I patronising? Oh no. Just envious. But we can't all have Lisa's advantages.

The Times
26 September 1998

27

One Man: the Reasons Why

I include, with scant apologies, a second piece about a second well-beloved grey horse. It is here because it takes on a different subject as well as a different horse. With the Dessie piece, I pondered on the nature of public love that flows towards a special horse. In this piece, I take up the question of why it is that we put our beloved horses through the terrible stresses of competition.

It is a question at the heart of the matter. The horse called One Man was killed in the Grand National; and it was a terrible thing. Should he have been spared it then? Do we have a right to put any horse, let alone a beloved horse such as this, through such an ordeal? I have tried here to give something of an answer.

Tragedy. A great media word: though one that media people are sometimes a little shy of. They don't want to use it if the event they speak of is merely sad: they want to reserve it for events that are really most dreadfully sad.

But then, as I watched a video about the life and times of the big grey horse, One Man, we began, right at the start, with the statement that his death was tragic.

One Man was certainly a very splendid racehorse. He won Boxing Day's traditional firework display, the King George VI Chase, twice. He might have been going for a Desert Orchid-chasing hat-trick today had he not taken that fatal – tragic? – tumble at Aintree in the spring.

He won the Hennessy and also the Queen Mother Champion Chase at the Cheltenham Festival. He was some horse: but more than that. He was one of those rare beloved horses. He was not quite Dessie, but he excited the same quality of love.

He was grey, and that always helps. Recognising 'your' horse without the commentator's help is one of the pleasures of racing. And he was big and he was bold and he was sometimes outrageous in his jumping. Normally, the untrained must take this on trust, but you need never have seen a horse in your life to work out that One Man, taking off outside the wings and landing beyond the wings on the other side, was more than a little special. Damn near had wings himself.

And, of course, he was flawed. There is something about a brilliant but flawed horse that excites the protective instinct in those who watch.

One Man would occasionally put in a disastrous jump, and took one or two spectacular purlers in his career. At other times, he missed his chance of victory with a near-miss error, staying on his feet but knocking the stuffing out of himself with a botched leap. He never won the Gold Cup. Some thought that the fierce finish was a hill too far. But others thought it was lack of character. When it got really tough, he packed it in.

This is the sort of accusation that pains a loving owner more than any attack on himself. I remember administering the most terrible wigging – in the gents, of all places – to a person who publicly impugned the character of a horse of mine.

And John Hales, a toy-maker a good deal burlier even than his beloved burly horse, was an owner besotted; still incapable of speaking of his horse without a catch in his voice. And thereby lies the question at the heart of all the horsey sports.

It is a question that baffles the non-horsey; and so it should. It baffles the horsey just as much. If you love the horse so much, why put him in a position of danger? Why do you put him in a position that might cause him injury, or death? How could you?

Watching the video, it is hard to see where the owner's pleasures come from. We see Hales watching a race, or rather, not watching. He simply couldn't bear to.

We see him, eyes averted from the track, face contorted with stress and worry, an expression of utter misery, as if he were watching his daughter being sold at an auction for white slaves.

'Are they on the second circuit?' he asked. 'I mean, they are on the second circuit?' And at last the end of the race would come and put him out of his misery, taking him – sometimes, often, 20 times in 35 starts – to transcendent joy. And relief, as much as anything else.

But at Aintree in spring it was, alas, One Man who was put out of his misery: broken leg, the screens, the vet, the tears. Tragedy struck, said one report.

Tragedy cast a giant shadow. And so on. Any horse's untimely death diminishes us, if we have horsey blood in our veins. And that of a good one strikes twice as hard.

Tragedy is a term borrowed from drama, and a real tragedy has something dramatic about it. There is something terribly appropriate about a truly tragic death. Please note that I use the word 'terribly' to mean something to do with terror.

And there is a terrible drama about the death of a good horse. One Man was brought down by his tragic flaw, or one of them: his sometimes cavalier attitude to jumping, his sometimes too cocksure faith in his own ability to take wing.

Perhaps there was an added irony – for tragedies have ironies, while horrors and disasters do not – in that it was his courage that undid him. His courageous jumping was his hallmark, his most satisfying quality: and it killed him.

The video spares us the horrors. But we do see the two failed attempts at the Gold Cup, when it was transparently obvious that he was blocked, not by his lack of stomach for the fight, but by lack of stamina.

He seemed almost bewildered as he changed in about four strides from Pegasus to Dobbin. But at a shorter distance, preferably without a killing hill, he sprouted wings, and the hearts of the horsey world flew with him. He gave huge joy, and it killed him.

Why put him through it? Why not leave him in a nice paddock with his head down eating grass? Isn't that what he wants? It is like the human dream of the good life: Caribbean beach and a drink with an umbrella in it. But after a week – call it 24 hours – you would be dying a slow death of pure boredom.

Humans have a need to rejoice in their talents, to express them. We climb mountains, play football, seek promotion, walk with lions; we seek out challenges, rather than avoid them. The drink with the umbrella in it doesn't taste any good without the challenges that preceded it.

I suspect it is the same for the sweet grass of the paddock. A horse has its natural being in movement and dominance and the avoidance of predators: and for a horse to live in perfect peace is – well, a bit like living in sheltered accommodation. If it comes too early in life, it is not a life-enhancer: it is a life-destroyer.

The horsey sports work because horses embrace them: humans and horses meet across the barrier of species in these wild moments of shared risk, shared fulfilment. There was indeed something of the tragedy in the death of One Man. Something altogether worth savouring: a great horse, who gave the lot.

There is a line from a tragedy that encompasses practically all of the horsey sports: then, must you speak of one that loved not wisely but too well.

The Times
26 December 1998

28

Sheikh Mo (Part Two)

This is another scant-apologies piece. But Sheikh Mohammed and his Godolphin racing operation is a bigger subject than most in racing. And I confess, I have found something irresistible about the sheikh's irresistible urge for conquest: and in his genuine sportsmanship.

I made the trip to Dubai to watch the world endurance riding championship, in which Sheikh Mohammed took part, riding 100 miles across the desert. I also went to pay a visit to the racehorses. It was a few days of heat and horses: and ambition.

Forget about the money. If you want to understand Sheikh Mohammed, if you want to understand Godolphin, the most extraordinary phenomenon in world racing, you must stop being impressed by money. Hard, I know, but being impressed by Godolphin money is like looking at a Formula One car and being impressed by the petrol.

You can't understand the money. So don't even try. It is like understanding distance. I can understand the distance between my house and Newmarket. I can understand the distance between Newmarket and Dubai. I can, if I try very hard, understand the quarter-million miles from Dubai to the moon.

I can even, just about, get my head around the 93 million miles – the eight light-minutes – between the earth and the sun. But when it comes to the distance in light-years between our galaxy and the Horsehead nebula,* then I am all at sea.

So it is with a sheikh's billion billions. So just don't think about it: it will only make you ill. Savour, instead, the tangible. Horses. And ambition: ambition that seems to be as solid as the horses dozing in their boxes.

Godolphin is Sheikh Mohammed's personal spaceship, from which he has set out to boldly go where no racehorse owner has gone before. The horses winter in Dubai, in the gorgeous, warm, dry heat of the desert, and the best of them come to Newmarket to conquer Europe in the spring and summer.

Turn off the Abu Dhabi freeway, away from the coastal line of buildings, and the tone of the land changes at once into desert sepia. And there, surreal, a cricket match: the flannelled men poised as the bowler runs in; white on brown, the colour balance all wrong.

And then, turning into a gate, like entering the Tardis. The inside seems to be much bigger than the outside and, certainly,

* I learnt after writing this that the Horsehead nebula is in fact in the Milky Way, our own galaxy. Still, you see what I mean, I hope . . .

the transformation is as staggering, as unexpected. Suddenly, we are in the lush green cool, a sheikh's oasis for his horses.

The horses are in various stages of preparation in the long, cool barns. Morning exercise with a fleet of work riders, many of them European. The careful cosseting attention of the grooms. And green grass and the blue livery of Godolphin in the paddock sheets that horses wear as they cool down after a morning charge across the desert sand.

The names beside the boxes are a Who's Who of racing animals. But then a small double-take: there's High-Rise – but he wasn't a Godolphin horse when he won the Derby, was he? And there is Xaar, who was, for a few brief weeks last spring, the latest contender for Horse of the Century before his defeat in the 2,000 Guineas. He wasn't a Godolphin horse then, either.

But they are Godolphin animals now – and racing is not quite sure how to deal with this. Some people definitely resent a sheikh impudently buying up all the opposition. 'People think we just buy up good horses,' Simon Crisford, the Godolphin racing manager, said, 'but we see a very good horse we can make even better. With the right training, the right campaign. It is another challenge.'

It is an example of thinking in financial light-years, a way of thinking that is dazzling to those of us whose purses operate on comprehensible distances. 'The winter in Dubai is a proving ground, a testing ground,' Crisford said. 'There are just 60 places on that plane to Newmarket. Only the best horses will make the trip.'

A high failure rate is inevitable and here is the point: no one else in racing can think like this. Here is an interesting twist: a good 20 or so of the horses that do make the trip won't be going to England to race; they will be there as gallop schoolmasters. They are horses of considerable quality whose job it will be to work alongside the budding stars of the next campaign.

All racing yards have such work companions, but no trainer will tell you their names. This is because the work horses are also racehorses, being trained to win races, paid for by an owner who might not be best pleased at the mildly demeaning role played by his own particular darling. But a sheikh can please himself because his financial considerations are on a different planet.

We will never get to see Godolphin's books, but you wonder how much of it is the sheikh's folie de grandeur – which is how most of the world sees the Godolphin operation – and how much is based on hard financial sense.

Perhaps Godolphin operates by the same rules as the rest of us, but on a scale so different that no one can quite get the hang of it. Certainly, the sale of the great Lammtarra for £30 million points out the ancient business truth – it is never wrong to take a profit.

Newmarket is Newmarket and it always feels like the centre of the universe when you are there. There is no town but Newmarket and no racing but English racing. And Godolphin's European headquarters is, of course, Newmarket. Yet, out in Dubai, the great, green heath seems, well, light-years away. In Dubai, you can look around in all kinds of different directions. All over the world, in fact.

Godolphin is increasingly looking beyond its own dreams of dominance of English racing. It is looking to conquer the entire planet. 'Worldwide racing,' Crisford said. 'That is the aim of this operation. And it always has been, right from the moment we began.'

And that, again, is thinking on a scale to which no one else in racing can aspire: not the odd raider here and there, but a solid global programme of goals and targets and races with the entire planet as your home paddock.

It makes sense, or at least it does if you have the hottest streak of ambition in racing. It also makes sense financially, as English racing may be among the best in the world but it is also among the poorest.

Understanding the nature and scope of a sheikh's ambition is tough work and most people don't even try. Dubai offers a better clue than Newmarket and you can sense it in the quiet of the Tardis Oasis. At the quiet time in the horsey year, the horses dozing as the desert sun sinks below the horizon, you get a better idea of the nature of it.

In the peace of the yard, you feel the purpose behind it all. Behind it all, the presence of a man who is seeking something a little more than victory. Sheikh Mohammed has, after all, known plenty of victories. He is seeking to explore limits: the limits of what is possible in horse racing.

The audacity of his ambition is matched by the coolness of the planning and the gentleness of the atmosphere at these times of dozing content. Sheikh Mohammed is not trying to bag a few peaks, he is seeking to explore human and equine possibilities, in the because-it-was-there sense of the first climbers of Everest, the first four-minute miler, the first men on the moon.

He wants to explore the boundaries of the possible, to set records and then to beat them himself. Himself.

The Times
9 January 1999

29

A Triumph

Most able-bodied people have a problem with disabled people. It is not because they are nasty people, but because they feel a sense of embarrassment, a feeling of not knowing what to say. I have now done several horsey stories with disabled people: utterly without embarrassment. The first reason for this is the lack of embarrassment felt by the people themselves: and that is contagious. If they are matter-of-fact and down-to-earth and free of self-pity, you are not going to be tongue-tied and full of pity yourself.

But then, you see, there is always something to talk about. And this is horses. There is no better conversational gambit in life than 'tell me about your horse'. And once the degree of intimacy has been established, a lot of things become easy.

Meeting Debbie was one of the greatest privileges I had in the process of assembling material for this book.

You can always find people who prefer rules to common humanity; you can always find people who think that the best way to deal with something uncomfortable is to look the other way. All of which brings us to Debbie Criddle: a quiet, composed person not given to making a fuss. And we come also to a collector's item of a case: a sporting organisation admitting a mistake. What is more, a sporting organisation backing down, making hurried and important changes.

Most of the people I write about in this column have riding abilities so far away from mine that it can be measured in light-years. Criddle is better than me by, say, 93 million miles: the distance from the earth to the sun. That is to say, this distance is unbridgeable, but it is comprehensible.

To convert to football, Criddle is a very good non-league player, probably up there in the Nationwide Conference; I am languishing in one of those leagues that doesn't get its results printed in the Sunday papers. But I can do more than admire what she does with a horse. I can also relate to it.

One slight difference: Criddle has only one functioning arm. The other day, I was asked to ride with only one hand on the reins. This mean and simple exercise shows you how much you rely on your hands, how little your seat and legs – supposedly where the real power and control come from – are actually contributing. I found my horse was failing even to go round corners.

Criddle, 32, from Somerset, rides with her right arm strapped up, to stop it swinging about. She also has a problem with her right leg, which is sometimes a mite slow to obey its mistress. To be centred on a horse – and dressage, like any other kind of riding, is all about being centred, balanced and even – she must ride in a delicately twisted position. This makes everything a good deal more difficult.

In dressage, in all kinds of riding, precise control of the horse is a function of your own understanding, plus the precise control of your own body. Criddle wanted to ride dressage at regional and national level. As the Irishman said to the person asking directions: 'If I were you, I wouldn't start from here.' So she did it. Last year, she took her horse to the regional finals, competing against able-bodied people. 'It was my goal,' she said. 'It was the year my dream came true.'

So, two weeks ago, a new addition to the British Dressage rule-book stated that riders must have both hands on the reins at all times. This has always been the case – but this time, no dispensations were allowed at regional and national level. You want to compete, get back to your disabled ghetto. It was an absolutely shattering blow.

Criddle is not a lifelong horsey person. At 19, she was busy, ambitious, fulfilled in her professional life, working for a builder's merchant. Then came a motorcycle accident. It was one of those fifty-fifty cases; she recovered mostly because she wanted to live. And horses became the structure of her daily life, and her ambition. Horses do not look away in distaste at an injury. Horses are judgemental, yes, but they judge you on what you are, on how you treat them, how you relate to them. Horses judge; they do not prejudge. They are sentient creatures without prejudice.

The same is not true of all horse people. However, this is not the moment to trumpet injustice, because British Dressage changed its rule at breakneck speed. Disabled people are now allowed to compete with a special dispensation.

There are some who believe that the notion of the dispensation itself is demeaning and unnecessary, but that is another matter. It is tempting to lay into the people who caused such dismay and distress, but I shall bite my lip. Instead, let me congratulate British Dressage for having the moral courage to back down. This is generally a good deal harder than sticking to your guns.

I met Criddle when she went for a training session at the legendary Talland School of Equitation in Gloucestershire. Leaning against her car as she changed into riding gear, left hand – she was born right-handed – and teeth doing the job, precise and matter-of-fact. We talked riding technicalities and the special difficulties that she has with flying changes.

The flying change is a move that, as it were, separates the men from the boys in dressage. If a horse and rider can perform a series of flying changes, they are more than just good. Within half an hour, Criddle was riding flying changes every second stride – 'twos', in the jargon – which is something she had never even tried before. It was glorious stuff. Improvement: training on. And, no, not to prove yourself or to prove a point. It is the notion of going forward. It is the most exciting thing in the horsey world.

The notion of 'bringing on' a horse in any of the disciplines is intoxicating. To take a horse and to improve it and to prove the improvement in competition: there is no greater joy, no matter at what level or what discipline you compete. Sheikh Mohammed bought the Derby winner last year because he thought he could improve it. The desire to improve, to kick on, is at the absolute heart of the business.

There is obviously an aspect of personal development in all this. I remember being told that a once promising young man had never fulfilled his potential as a trainer 'mostly because he never really trained on as a human being'.

Criddle has certainly trained on herself. A fulfilled life, a family, horses, ambitions. Of course, there are many ways of changing and fulfilling your life. Criddle happened to choose horses. Horses respond to skill and understanding and kindness. They make up their own minds about people and they don't care for anybody's opinion but their own.

Lesson over, Criddle changed from riding boots, putting on her lace-ups with skilled, unembarrassed movements of fingers and teeth.

'And one of the small extra pleasures is that it doesn't even hurt when I'm riding,' she said. 'It hurts most of the time, but when I'm riding, I'm concentrating so much on everything else, that the pain doesn't get through.' Spoken quite matter of factly, as if constant pain was part of everybody's life. It is my belief that people in sport should crawl on their knees across broken glass and beg at the feet of people like Criddle; beg her to honour them by taking part in their competitions.

But let's write it off as a misunderstanding. Better that way. They just didn't expect anybody to be quite as good as Criddle: good enough to compete against able-bodied people at a serious level of competition. Moral: don't underestimate people like Debbie Criddle. 'I sometimes wonder what would happen if I could wave a magic wand and be like I was before the accident,' she said from the top deck of the horse on which she had so majestically performed her twos, her flying changes. 'And I think – well, perhaps I wouldn't have all this.' Just lucky, I suppose.

The Times
20 February 1999

30

A Victory

This is perhaps my favourite piece in the collection. I shall never forget the kindness of the household, and the slow dawning of understanding as I realised what this strange and daft story was really all about. If any story in this book gets anywhere near the heart of the horsey life, it is this one.

Quixall Crossett is the worst horse in racing. 'Well, he isn't,' Ted Caine, his owner, trainer, work-rider and mucker-outer said. 'People like to say that, but he isn't.' Just the 87 races so far in his career.

And he has not won a single one of them. He'll probably be having another crack over the Easter weekend.

There has never been such a bad racehorse, in terms of figures, anyway. The previous worst was Amrullah, with 74 successive defeats.

Quixall Crossett has taken losing into a new dimension.

He lives with three almost equally dodgy horses in the North Yorkshire Moors: start from Middlesbrough and take a road that goes winding between the tops and hang a left into High Crossett Farm. Fine spring morning, lapwings dancing their courting dance in the sky above.

Caine is a permit trainer, has been for 20 years, barring a single year out of the game. Permit trainers have a licence to train their own animals. He has had a nice horse here and there in his time: Cavalier Crossett won eight times – 'but that was a once-in-a-lifetime, that was'.

Quixall Crossett, however, runs and runs and never wins. And neither Ted nor his wife, Joy, will hear a word against him. They will, when pressed, admit that he is a little on the slow side, 'but he always quickens up towards the end of a race. You'll see.' So the video cranks into operation. A narrow-bodied bay, jockey in purple sleeves, and leading. That's Quixall – but the favourite passes him as if he was stuck in second and cruises 20 lengths ahead.

Ah, but wait, wait, wait for that famous second wind.

And Quixall starts to eat into the lead, stride by stride. And the Caines watch, rapt. How many times have they watched this video, how many times have they been rapt? They are in their fifties, eyes shining with the naive delight of it all. Two out and a terrible jump by the leader, the jockey staying on by happy or unhappy chance. An audible sigh from Joy: if you watch this video enough, surely one time the leading jockey might just slide – painlessly, of course, not an ounce of malice in this household – to the floor.

Even at the last, the leader puts in a poor jump and Quixall is behind him, jumping neatly and accurately. Come on, Quixall!

But no, the winning post comes, Quixall has lost again. Only by two lengths, and second place isn't bad, and Quixall has been placed 18 times, and has been second once before, and there's glory for you.

The Caines bred Quixall themselves, a stallion fee of £50. He was named for Albert Quixall, the footballer: 'He was a blond inside forward and so was I.' Quixall the footballer joined Manchester United after the Munich air crash; Quixall the horse joined the Caines 14 years ago.

'Such big feet he had,' Joy said. 'It was as if all his strength had gone to his feet. It was like he had wellington boots on.'

'I was really pleased with the name,' Ted said, 'and I kept wishing I'd saved it for a good 'un.' A walk round the yard does not take long: a run of four roomy boxes, all occupied, with Quixall in the star's box by the entrance. Where do you exercise them? 'We just do bits round the farm. Up on the moors. Sometimes we go to the beach.'

There is a real, well, niceness about the pair of them, their uninhibited pleasure in their horses. They are far from humourless: they take a shy delight in Quixall's burgeoning celebrity status. Quixall gets his own fan mail. A typical example applauded his sterling efforts and had a couple of quid Sellotaped to the card: 'Ask Mr Caine to spend this on carrots for you.' But still I didn't understand.

Many people would have got rid of the wellington-booted Quixall, but the Caines believed that he would improve (he could hardly go the other way, after all) and at just about the age of nine he grew into himself. In Flat racing, a late developer is one that matures in the autumn rather than spring of his three-year-old season, but the Caines are as generous with their time as they are with the cheese and malt loaf.

They have taken other dodgy horses, horses that no one else wants. 'We've taken them out of the rubbish bin.' One of the four, Triona's Hope, was a chronic rearer when he came to them; no longer. What did you do to cure him? 'Nothing really. Just bits around the farm. A bit of time. No pressure.' Quixall is a decent, sensible horse that can jump. He is the right sort of animal to be schoolmaster to an apprentice, or easy companion to an amateur. So they run the horse mostly in apprentice and amateur races, which is also cheaper. It is a good deal all round. 'And you don't give up when he's enjoying himself,' Caine said. 'We will keep going as long as he likes it. He jumps round, he enjoys it and he comes back sound because he knows how to look after himself. So we think about the next race.'

But what about that year off, why did he give up training for a year? 'Oh, that was when our son was killed.' A sweet and friendly smile. 'I didn't feel like training then, but I took out a licence again the following year.' Malcolm, their son, was killed in an accident on the farm; Malcolm who was going to take the place over, in the fullness of time.

Joy was the one who found him. Devastation such as this destroys the survivors – but the Caines have not been destroyed. 'Well, it was Quixall that kept us going, really.' And suddenly this dotty pilgrimage around the racecourses of the North makes sense.

Suddenly I can understand the delight in the occasional place, the real pride in the two seconds. 'We enjoy going to the races more than ever,' Caine said, 'and we'll keep going. As long as he likes it.' And it becomes clear that Quixall Crossett has seen the Caines through a period of the most unspeakable grief. Life: that is what horses are good at. That is what horses give. Also, they require so much looking after, what with feeding and watering and mucking out and exercising, that, even in despair, you have the business of life to deal with: the lives of the horses in your hands, their life-affirming nature to live with, the sound of munching in the dark, the whickering as the feed bucket clangs in the yard, the feel of horse beneath you at morning exercise.

And so the Caines take Quixall to the races, again and again, and he gives the amateur a nice day out and the apprentice a good lesson and it is all pure gold for the Caines. 'He's not fast,' Caine conceded, albeit reluctantly, 'but he's a survivor.' And so are they: kind people with a horse of almost impossible generosity. Quixall has had 87 races without victory. Quixall and the Caines are undefeated.

The Times
27 March 1999

31

Horse-whispering (Part Two)

Monty Roberts has rather divided the horse world: his horse-whispering methods go against the grain of tradition, and much of the horse world depends on tradition; suspects deeply anything that has not been done before. There is great hostility to him; one magazine once told me: 'You can write about anything you like so long as it is not Monty Roberts.'

The new methods do not provide an answer to absolutely everything: rather, they provide a new approach to ancient problems. It is a new way of thinking. We do too much without thought in our horsey lives, because that is the way we have been taught, the way it has always been done.

I don't want to over-sell Monty; nor do I wish to undervalue him. I am a supporter, without being a disciple. There is much in what he says: and anyone who refuses to listen is daft. Any horse person who refuses to listen is doing himself a disservice.

After my two days with Monty, I spent the following weekend working with one of his disciples: doing a weekend course in join-up with Kelly Marks. After watching Monty at work, you are naturally itching to try it yourself: by working with Kelly I was able to do exactly that – and do it right.

MONTY

Humans have lived with horses for 8,000 years. Horses were essential. Horses were what made things move. Horses were people-movers, carriers of burdens, the power behind agriculture – and horses were needed to fight wars. War was the horse's prime function in human life.

Yet, in the past 50 years, everything has changed. Horses are for pleasure. They give us the greatest sport on earth and the jolliest amateur and children's events. They give us the unending non-competitive pleasures of horsemanship. We no longer have horses because we must. We have horses because we want to. We keep horses – the racehorses of Newmarket, the gymkhana ponies, the riding school hacks, the show ponies, my own beasts – for love.

And, as brute necessity no longer colours our relationship with horses, so it is time for a new covenant between our two species. And it is happening, all over the world. This country is on the cutting edge.

It is no longer revolutionary; it is well on the way to becoming mainstream and the movement's leader was back in England yet again, packing 'em in as ever. Monty Roberts, the real horse whisperer. A term that he loathes.

A high-stepping hackney stallion and a big Californian man, 64, with a flat cap over his eyes; also an audience of 1,300 crammed into Towerlands equestrian centre in Essex. The horse wouldn't get on a lorry without two hours of pulling and poking and prodding and whacking. Enter Monty.

Twenty minutes later, the stallion was walking on to the lorry by himself. It looked like a miracle. Roberts, a great showman, knows perfectly well that he looks like a miracle-worker. Most people would be content to bask in the glory of this. 'I have no special skill,' he said. Again and again. 'I am not a genius.'

Roberts does not want to be seen as a one-off, a freak genius, a horse whisperer. He says that anybody can do it. He has wider ambitions than being a genius. He would prefer to be a prophet. He wants to be seen as the man who changed for ever the way in which horses and human beings relate to each other. He is a big man of colossal passions and no one can watch him work with horses without wonder.

Why did the hackney stallion walk up the ramp of the lorry on his own? Because he wanted to be with Roberts, preferred that to being away from him. This desire overcame his fear of the forbidding darkness of a lorry – for Roberts was on the lorry.

Why did the horse want to be with Roberts. Magic? No. Much more interesting than that. Horses communicate with body language. So Roberts uses the body language that the horses understand best of all: horsey body language. He gets the horses to think of him as a fellow horse. His body language tells them that he represents not an invasive and frightening predator but companionship, comfort, security. Thus a horse that has never had a saddle, still less a human on his back, can be ridden away in half an hour. This is Roberts's more or less daily miracle. He has started – he hates the term 'broken' – nearly 11,000 horses in this way.

His first book, *The Man Who Listens to Horses*, is more or less a Freudian textbook, with a violent abusive father who beat his sons and his horses without distinction. Roberts observed herds of feral horses and had a life-changing experience in watching an interaction between a dominant mare and an uppity young male.

He adapted what he saw to training horses without violence, seeing, with a leap of insight, that a human could take the place of that mare. This remained an obscure and more or less private miracle until the Queen asked him to come to England to work with her horses. Since then, the Roberts methods have spread ever wider.

'How can we apologise to this species for our 8,000 years of mistreatment?' he asked his audience with a theatrical flourish. He stood a distance away from the young horse that he had just started and asked the audience to clap. A crash of applause. The horse, alarmed, ran straight to the security of Roberts's side.

Cruelty distresses him. Mistrust distresses him still more. He is a man haunted by betrayal, a tale told in every page of that first book. The traumas of his own life have been given validity by his desire to heal the wounds of betrayal between Homo and Equus.

'I was chosen by the horses,' he says in his more grandiloquent moments, and Roberts has many of these. I spent two days with the Roberts roadshow. We sat quietly watching the horses that he was to work with the following evening, talking about horses. He showed me how rapid movement of the eyes alarms a horse; for that is what a predator does. 'I never snap my eyes. I slide them.'

He likes to get a feel of his audience. 'Raise your hands if you own a horse.' A good 70 per cent. 'Raise your hands if you are professionally involved with horses.' Fewer than 1 per cent.

There is great resistance to Roberts as well as a great attraction. Roberts is a threatening presence to some. Others, professionally involved with many animals, simply do not have time to rethink the philosophy of life: it would be like U-turning on a motorway.

This is a grass-roots revolution and it is happening under the noses of the professionals. And professionals, more slowly, are turning to it, mostly in desperation with problem horses, because traditional methods have failed. It is becoming increasingly obvious that the Roberts methods are quicker and safer, as well as kinder. Nothing that works – nothing that saves time, nothing that saves good and valuable horses – can be dismissed.

And there is Roberts filling the interval with signing and questions and doing the same after the performance. The man is a reckless spendthrift of himself. His willingness, his eagerness to reach out for people and touch them reminds me a little of Muhammad Ali. He has a gift of intimacy without ever quite ceasing to be a public person. And always driven: driven to perform, to explain, to demonstrate, to talk, to advise. 'I have a horse that's whip-shy.' 'Then go back to your yard and make a bonfire and get out all your whips . . .'

There are plenty of tales of cruelty, but to concentrate on them is to miss the point. In the new world of the pleasure horse, there is not a vast amount of genuine cruelty. But our manners are really rather coarse. It is time to change that.

The Times
17 April 1999

KELLY

Last week I wrote about a genius: Monty Roberts, the real horse whisperer. Last weekend, all that he did, I did myself. I became a horse whisperer: a genius, if you prefer. Everybody else on the course became a genius as well. It was an astounding couple of days.

Roberts has become an evangelist and in his roadshow he will perform four miracles a night. He will prepare a young horse to be ridden away in 30 minutes, a slight improvement on the usual eight weeks. He will take a horse that refuses to enter a lorry and have him walking in and out of a lorry of his own choice. And so on.

'Anybody can do it,' Roberts says. And I am now in a position to prove him 100 per cent right. I was invited to join one of the Intelligent Horsemanship courses run by Kelly Marks, the only courses fully endorsed by Roberts.

Marks is a former jockey and was the women's champion on the Flat in 1995. 'I couldn't imagine anything in life giving me the satisfaction of race-riding,' she said – but chance intervened and she joined up with Roberts in, of all places, a French petrol station. That changed the direction of her life.

Join-up is at the heart of all this whispering business, but let us get whispering sorted out before we go any further. Everybody involved in the Monty Roberts techniques hates the term 'horse whisperer'. For a start, the film of that name was a travesty of the Roberts methods and employed the very cruelties that motivated him to find his alternative approach.

Yet the term had a vogue, largely because it strikes a deep chord in human beings. We like the idea of a magician, a genius, a person so strange and wild and singular that he can, indeed, speak to horses. He is something nobody else is: a shaman, a witch doctor, a man who can converse with the beasts. We dearly want that to be true. Which makes me a shaman and a witch doctor myself, of course.

The truth of the matter is that everyone involved with horses is a horse whisperer. We all seek to communicate with our animals and must take responsibility for our actions. When it comes to communicating with animals, there is no higher power than oneself. The myth of the horse whisperer is based on funk, on abnegation of responsibility.

Roberts is no genius, not in the sense that horses respond to him in a unique fashion. His genius was in observation of the way in which horses behave in the wild and, especially, in translating that into human terms. It provides the basis of a new and easier way of working with horses.

Cut, then, to a dozen people wandering about sheepishly in a round wire pen, throwing lunge-lines at each other, fixing each other with steely eyes and making mad sort of Gary Glitter gestures at each other. We were walking through join-up, taking it in turns to be the horse. Beneath the light dressing of jokes, there was an atmosphere of deadly seriousness: we would all be doing it for ourselves very soon, each one on our own in a round pen with a horse. It was slightly important to know what to do.

Fast forward to Sunday afternoon: and there I am, leading a burly black hackney mare into a round pen, the eyes of the course upon me. Unclip the horse from the lunge-line and at once the horse spins. And I send her away, just as, 40-odd years ago, Roberts saw the boss mare of a wild herd send away a naughty young colt.

I sent my horse away with aggressive eye contact and confrontational body language. Emphasising my control, I sent the horse in the opposite direction, by means of eye contact and strong body language. I kept him at it, running around me in circles, with flicks of the lunge-line – a soft cotton line that cannot cause pain. The communication took place in equine, not in human terms, you see.

Then I caused the horse to change direction once again and, by this time, her inside ear was cocked towards me, telling me she was listening to me. Her lips began to chew, telling me that she wished to graze; could she please rejoin the safety of the herd and come and graze in proper horsey companionship.

I am not a horse, but she asked me to be her security. And therein lies the miracle, the change of attitude, the new covenant between horse and human. How could I refuse? Her circles were closer to me now and then she bowed her head, stating strongly her wish to graze. And I changed. I dropped the Gary Glitter stuff, lowered my eyes, turned away and assumed a slightly hunched position, indicating relaxed and complete passivity. This meant: you may join me now, if you wish. She wished. She stopped, took a step towards me. I gave her a rub of acknowledgement. Then I turned away and went passive again.

And she joined up. Just like that. I walked briskly away, and she followed. I changed direction, she changed direction. Wherever I went, I had a big black velvet nose about an inch from my shoulder. I stopped and praised her and rubbed her.

And, from there, I went on to put a saddle and a bridle on her and legged a rider on to her back. This was not a new experience for her; it was me, not her, that was supposed to be learning. And then, at the end of it all, I untacked her and led her back. Not without a quiet word of thanks.

What on earth is the use of this kind of stuff? Many a conventional horse person has asked the same thing. 'Ideas like this traditionally pass through three stages,' Marks said. 'First ridicule, then hostility, then general acceptance.' The hostility gets greater as these ideas find wider acceptance.

What use? The horse that refuses to get on a lorry is probably the most common behavioural problem in horsemanship. As chance would have it, Marks had promised to help with a horse that had not been on a trailer for two years. The horse had to be ridden to the yard, the trailer came separately.

The owner has a tale to tell. She sent the horse to a proper, approved riding establishment for reschooling. Her bill included the cost of two schooling whips that had been broken across her horse's back. Getting off the trailer from that establishment was the last time the horse had been near any form of horse transport. It took Marks 20 minutes to put right the hurts of two years. You simply cannot argue with a technique that can do such a thing.

Marks can teach humans as well as horses. She is teaching – and teaching with great effectiveness – a technique that opens the door to better, easier and safer horsemanship; and more satisfying horsemanship, too. Never mind whispering, this is something worth bellowing about.

The Times
24 April 1999

32

'Four-in-hand' Barnes

I had always rather fancied the idea of driving – and been rather alarmed by it. The tacking up, for a start, looks like one of the most terrifying exercises in all of horsemanship: and slightly disastrous if you get it wrong.

Then there is the fact that you are not directly in contact with the horse, that if things go wrong, you are quite helpless. And then there is the problem that you are dealing with multiples of horse: and as everyone who has sat on a horse knows, it is hard enough trying to control one.

Driving is regarded by some people as something of a soft option: riding with the heat taken off. Well, riding with four in hand is one of the more challenging and exhilarating tasks in the horsey world. I thought it was great.

The gap looked a bit tight to me. 'Are we going to make this?'

'No problem. You could drive a horse and carriage through there.' And so I proceeded to drive a horse and carriage through there, hitting neither the tree on my left nor the Range Rover on my right.

The team of four Welsh ponies ahead of me, their hooves ringing on the Tarmac in brief staccato pony rhythm, and I felt one of those power surges, like the sort that blows your computer, going through the entire team, and for a moment I thought I might lose the lot of them and be off bowling through Windsor without any control whatsoever.

There is a character in *The Forsyte Saga* called Swithin 'Four-in-Hand' Forsyte. Well, I plan to change my byline to Four-in-Hand Barnes. I asked the team to come back to me, and being wonderfully schooled animals, they overcame their doubts about my uncertain and unfamiliar touch and paid proper attention. And balanced and straight and controlled and purposeful, we turned back towards Windsor Castle.

'Good ponies,' I told them. We passed other carriages along the way, for this was one of the sport's big meetings, which is also, of course, a gathering of the clans. After an hour or so, this seemed not only natural, but inevitable: the occasional motor vehicle the eccentric and untoward intruder. I was with Georgina Frith, who is at Windsor this weekend to compete in the Asprey and Garrard International Driving Grand Prix. The structure of carriage driving events is based on the ridden three-day event. Frith, 30 this year, has won the national championship five times and has won the European championship for the past two years.

She is, then, pretty serious about winning, for this is an intense and serious sport, like any sport worth doing. And winning a big competition will sometimes provide enough money to cover the costs of transporting a big lorry with five ponies – the team plus a pony in the number 12 shirt – plus a trailer containing two carriages.

The word amateur means love, as in amo, amas, amat. The word professional is normally used to mean an utterly serious, properly prepared approach; a talent you can bank on. Frith is both these things.

I arrived at the Royal Windsor showground in time to watch the tacking up. Horse people spend their lives buckling buckles; assembling a bridle from a cat's cradle of leather is the first nightmare assignment of the horse-mad child.

I think the key to carriage driving is that its demands depend on the geometrical, rather than arithmetical progression. That is to say, your problems are not added to each other; they are multiplied. Anything from tacking up to making them stop and go is not four times more difficult, but eight.

The tacking up takes for ever, even with Team Frith in full cry. She travels with two grooms, who are also, of course, in it for love. A groom's job involves not only looking after five beasts, but also acting as a kind of side-car passenger, hanging off the edge of the carriage during high-speed manoeuvres.

The horsey part of the team comprises two leaders, who go at the front and whose principal job is to look good, and the wheelers, the pair at the back who do most of the actual pulling. Most human organisations work on the same principle.

The carriage itself is a thing of beauty: solid steel throughout and designed for hard use across difficult terrain, including charging flat-out through the odd river.

Frith has been driving since she was 12. It is one of those family things; her father has always bred Welsh ponies for driving.

Bloodlines, as we see most weeks in this space, are very important things in the horsey world.

The thing about horses is herd dynamics. A horse on his own is one thing: horses all together are quite another. That is why loose horses jump the Grand National: for the love of company. A lot of riding is about persuading your horse to concentrate on you, rather than the presence, or for that matter the absence, of other horses. It is all about getting into the mind of the horse.

A team of four horses is a herd, and a good carriage driver is concentrating not just on one mind but on five – the individual mind of each member of the team, plus the corporate herd identity. You can communicate with each individual by adjusting the reins in your hand, one rein for each horse. And you can communicate with the lot by using the reins together.

And so, retaking the reins, Frith put us through a series of manoeuvres at speed, a chance for the grooms to do their stuff, too. The horse and carriage that looks so unwieldy becomes a precise and very swift device, turning with altogether unexpected sharpness: Frith braced in her seat, me clinging on, the grooms doing their side-car bit. This is serious, wonderful horsemanship: the controlling of four horses at speed, team of horses, team of humans working as one.

'You can do too much of this, it's not something you practise every day,' Frith said. 'They love it too much.' Because herds love to run together, and each one's exuberance feeds on the other's, and by the rule of geometric progression you have a lunacy factor of eight as the herd instinct runs hot and strong.

Back to a walk, cooling off, and Frith telling a horror story about being flung from the carriage and seeing it vanish into the distance: eventually catching the team up, unharmed, having bogged their carriage down in a muck heap.

And telling me of that terrifying feeling when you lose contact with the mouths and the minds of the team: that terrible lightening of your hands, which you can find when things go wrong in a ridden horse. But your contact with a driven horse is more tenuous, so much more distant. You are on a knife-edge of control the whole time. If things go wrong, they tend to go very badly wrong indeed.

And that, of course, is the attraction of it: this fascination with multiples of horsey minds, the long reaching out to touch and to seek the cooperation of the mind of the herd. It is because of this that driving, particularly the driving of a large team, is perhaps the most deeply horsey sport of them all.

Training horses as individuals is the basis of practically all the horsey sports. But horses are always more than individuals: they have their being in company. A horse in a field on his own pines for a horse to join him. A horse on his own is always incomplete.

But with a team of four, you touch the mind of the herd and that is, perhaps, the deepest part of the horse's being. And there was me, driving down the Long Walk with the chestnuts in bloom and Windsor Castle looking timeless, seeking to touch that still more timeless thing, the mind of the herd. There was me, four in hand. Horse people and horses can be so generous, you know.

The Times
15 May 1999

33

There but for the Grace of God . . .

PETA BECKETT (PART TWO)

I was having a beer in the competitors' tent at Badminton, kindly invited in by Mark Todd. I had just walked the cross-country course with him, savouring its dangers and gathering material for my Badminton preview. And someone said hallo, and I turned round straight into a zillion-megawatt grin.

I was so delighted that I wanted to take her in my arms, hug her soundly and kiss her on both cheeks. I did not do so. We were not actually on hugging terms. I felt, no doubt correctly, that one single previous meeting – a lovely morning, researching a piece for my Saturday horsey column – did not justify such forward behaviour.

Instead, I sketched out a kind of intention movement for an embrace: I placed my right hand on her left shoulder and grinned back. She was overwhelmingly lovely, you see. Not merely pretty, but possessing a much rarer gift, that of making you feel better about being alive.

We talked about her horse and her hopes for Badminton and I teased her about the beauty of her flying changes and her vaulting and she laughed and I laughed and – well, that was it, really. But I walked away from the tent with a bounce in my step and a rather daft smile lingering on my lips. Going out, I felt better pleased with life than I had going in.

Her name was Peta Beckett and she was killed in a fall at the Savernake Forest horse trials last weekend. She was thrown from her horse at a bounce fence. She rode for Great Britain in the world championships last year. She was 33, married, with two children. It is all rather too much.

Oh, it was a lovely morning I spent at her place, watching her ride her top horse, Watermark III, down at the bottom end of a water meadow, and she popped the horse over the stream a couple of times just for the hell of it, and then cantered a series of figures of eight, performing a flying change each time her two circles intersected. Very nice horsemanship, that. God's in his heaven, all's right with the world.

Back at the yard, she posed for some pictures, doing so with the smiling delight that makes a photographer's day. 'Do you want to see my vaulting?' she asked. 'Your what?' Peter Nicholls, the photographer, replied. For an answer, she took her feet out of the irons, scissored her long legs and suddenly she was sitting in the saddle facing the wrong way. Laughing, she performed a series of absurd gymnastics, spinning round and round in the saddle.

This revealed a streak of profound flakiness and provided an appropriately delightful finishing touch to the morning. It was a morning that summed up all that was good about the horsey life.

Badminton this year was a nightmare of mud and rain and falling riders, but Beckett got round all right, finishing twenty-first overall and eighth best-placed Briton. Everyone left Badminton heaving sighs of relief that the worst injuries to riders were collarbones and concussion, and that no horse was badly hurt either. We had all feared the worst.

But her death last weekend came from a clear sky and the only civilised reaction is to sniffle and hope that they will ban all bounce fences, ban all other kinds of fence, ban horse trials, ban horses.

And it is right to feel this way – and also, of course, wrong. Every aspect of the horsey life is dangerous and horse trials represent this truth in an extreme form. The intimate relationship between joy and risk is part of all the dangerous sports. The two things are so tightly intertwined that there is not a hope in hell of sorting them out.

But the thing is, with the horsey sports, that you find something you simply cannot get from a rock face, an engine, a rip-cord, a stretch of ocean or white water. You get that savage communication with another kind of mammal: the deep and devastating intoxication of understanding and trust across the species barrier. Horse trials are the most testing examination of this trust.

Horse people are not adrenaline junkies, like the people who take part in the 'extreme' sports. They are addicted instead to that savage sense of communication, to that exploration of the profoundly unknowable things at the heart of the nature of the horse. Risk is just a part of it, but it is inescapable.

No one in the horsey world will take Beckett's death lightly. The horsey world must continue to work – without ever permitting a shred of complacency – to minimise the dangers to riders and horses both, knowing that it can never eliminate risk.

And no, at heart we do not want to ban fences, or horse trials, or horses. We may as well seek to ban joy, or ban life. I am deeply familiar with this contradiction and at times, especially after very good horsey moments, I even think I am getting close to understanding it.

But not this week. This week all I can do is wish to God that this terrible thing had never happened. I'll leave understanding for another time.

The Times
19 May 1999

ONE THAT WALKED AWAY

I finally managed to make my contact for this story when I was covering the cricket World Cup at Lord's. Sue rang me on her mobile and reached my mobile: and at once I heard the clipclop of hooves. We talked merrily above this sound, and the horses went into a trot. Then one of them neighed: it was a splendid moment; quite cheered me up from an incomparably dull cricket match which, to make things worse, Australia were winning easily.

Sue welcomed my suggestion that I join her on her adventure: and I had a wonderful day of it. I was in the middle of covering Wimbledon when I went that following week: it was a very acceptable change of pace.

This was a great thing that Sue did. All of us who are involved with horses are by definition lucky. But there is no ducking the dangers, and to call Sue lucky doesn't even begin to cover the situation. Naturally, she wants to spread a bit of her luck around.

Three years ago, Sue Upton-Whitting came off her horse while riding in a particularly hair-raising form of sport called team-chasing. She broke her neck, spent three months immobile in Stoke Mandeville Hospital and months afterwards in a brace.

Tomorrow, she is scheduled to complete a ride from Edinburgh to London: 700 miles of roads and bridleways, some of them with the horse she broke her neck on. 'It wasn't her fault,' she said. That is, after all, the sort of thing that horse people say.

So I went to join her for a leg of her epic journey and the first horse I rode that day was the horse she broke her neck on. Well, it *wasn't* her fault and a kinder, sweeter mare you couldn't meet in a day's march. In fact, I didn't. Her name is Tilly.

The double-barrel of the Upton-Whitting name will give the wrong impression. She was brought up on a small farm just round the corner from Anne Hathaway's cottage in Stratford-upon-Avon, never had much money but she had a pony. When she was 16, she went on to work at the stables of Bill Shand Kydd, whose double-barrel does reflect a life of privilege. He trained racehorses and he liked to ride in team chases. And a lot of water flowed under a lot of bridges.

Shand Kydd is now 61, Upton-Whitting 47. Four years ago, Upton-Whitting's team took part in a team chase and won. Shand Kydd was there. And came off his horse and broke his neck. He was one who did not walk away. He is completely paralysed and needs a ventilator to breathe. He has said that his life would be changed beyond recognition if he was able to move his little finger.

Upton-Whitting knew that she ought to go and see her former boss, but kept putting it off, as you do. Then she ended up in Stoke Mandeville and she asked after him, found that he was still there and so was able to make her visit in somewhat altered circumstances. On Thursday, Shand Kydd did his bit to support the ride by making a tandem parachute jump out of an aeroplane, the first time that such a thing has been attempted by a tetraplegic.

The ride and the jump are stunts to raise money for the International Spinal Research Trust. Those who walk away from places such as Stoke Mandeville are frequently filled with a desperate need to do something for the cause: there but for the grace of God. 'It was seeing the children,' Upton-Whitting said – and needed to say no more. A poem from a paralysed child has touched her deeply: words of Emma Provan, who was left paralysed by a drunk driver. She is 11. 'But the accident shouldn't have happened,' she wrote, with heart-piercing directness.

So I joined Upton-Whitting for a day of joy and hilarity, one of those days sent from heaven, about 20 miles of Warwickshire countryside, merry people, merry horses, mile upon mile of bridleway between Stratford and Banbury, ending with a fast scamper up the side of the Cotswolds. You wouldn't want to fall off at that sort of clip, but we didn't and it was all simply glorious.

You don't need horses to break your neck, but you cannot deny that it helps. But you are more likely to do it in a traffic accident. Or falling off a ladder, for that matter. Riding a motorbike is always a good way to put yourself in the risk category. Those who take part in the risk sports always insist that the reason for doing it has nothing to do with a love of death: au contraire. It is a love of life and some of us are never more truly alive than when on the back of a nice horse.

Yet an uncomfortable number of the life-loving devotees of risk sports will need the help of the International Spinal Research Trust: skiers, climbers and, obviously, parachutists. Rugby players can also suffer spinal injuries, generally when there is a serious power and weight difference between opponents.

We stopped for a moment and I changed horses, this time to a sparky mare called, of all things, Rabbit. One of those restless mares who pull a bit and badly need to be in front. A bit of a handful and the sort of mare I always especially like.

Why don't we want easy, push-button horses, safe-as-houses horses, stop-and-go horses? Why don't we want point-and-kick machines? Because horses are alive.

For some of us, horses are life. And you really do feel quite fiercely alive as you soften your hands and seek an understanding, a communication, with the mare, with life.

Upton-Whitting spent years planning this dramatic jaunt. She has done it with four horses, swapping mounts at midway each day, riding with Rachel Winters and supported by a back-up crew of two. They have tapped into the network of horsey and farming people, slept in caravans, arranged an overnight field for the beasts. She and Winters got the horses racing-fit in time for the start and their desperate ambition is to arrive in London tomorrow with four sound, non-limping horses. This has been a task that has tested to the full talents of organisation and horsemanship. It has taken determination to set it up, and more of the same to go through with it.

Upton-Whitting is full of stories, naturally, for this has been a great adventure. Lost in a forest and making a four-hour detour. The time they got stuck in a bog – frightening, leg-breaking country. The time they hacked unknowingly across the set of *Emmerdale Farm*.

And always tales of people they have met, who have given them support and, of course, money. And the team tightly bonded and full of affection and jokes, a goal they desperately want to reach, a magical time they desperately don't want to end.

It has been for them an enchanted time and it was a privilege to be, for a short way, a part of it, a privilege to be a part of a noble cause, a great adventure and to have had such marvellous fun. Changing horses again, this time to a handsome dun who needed a rider in a Clint Eastwood poncho to look his best. And discussing why we did it: why horses, why face the financial ruination, the heartbreak, the very serious risk?

And I remembered Ian Stark, the three-day eventer, in Barcelona after his Olympic cross-country round, being asked the obligatory crass question of how it felt. 'There is nothing better in the world,' he said. 'Except maybe sex.'

Note that 'maybe'. It is for the Emma Provans of the world that Upton-Whitting is riding, for the, in every sense, helpless innocents – but she is also riding for the sheer joy of it and for all of us who ride for the sheer joy of it, knowing that our shared joys will always have that small piece of terrible risk.

And finally, riding the last couple of miles on a charming little mare, both of us full of a pleasant, righteous tiredness. And we turned the four horses out into their fields for the night and they rolled in full content and got their heads down and grazed. And a while later, the humans were having a stiff drink while the horses were munching on a good serious feed. They too had enjoyed it: how could they not? Life-loving, you see.

The Times
26 June 1999

34

An Afternoon as a Champion

I had a chance ride in this event the previous year, and said I would love to do it again – but I asked Sandy Thwaites, who was doing the PR, if she could come up with an angle that would make it a proper story. Unbelievably, she came up with a champion.

Last Sunday I was a star. People pointed me out as I passed. Looked knowingly at one another when I was near. Stood back to admire, came close to bask in the regal presence. Made little remarks to show their familiarity. They were, in short, mildly obsequious. Just as they should be, I think you'll agree.

'That's him,' they said. And with an air of modesty that only emphasised my incalculably lofty status, I agreed. Long-haired, slim, self-assured, tough, undeniably handsome, but also with an air of infinite ability; awe-inspiring certainly, but also possessed of a fundamental decency of heart; and 15 hands at the wither.

Oliver's Taboo: that was the one they turned their heads to adore. Olly: a star if ever there was one. But there was me riding him, riding him in competition, what's more. The occasion was the Petplan Festival of Endurance Riding, and I had been invited to ride in their 15-mile 'celebrity' event, competing for the *Horse & Hound* team. And out of her quite extraordinary generosity, Jo Trego lent me Olly for the day.

It was an honour, and the horse let me know it. Last time I set eyes on him, it was four o'clock on a desert morning in Dubai, the world endurance championship last December, with 100 miles of desert before him.

Four times, this quite incredible horse has won the 100-mile Golden Horseshoe event across Exmoor. He won a 75-mile event when part of a novice Great Britain team in Belgium. He won the national championship at Cirencester in 1994. He won the Qatar International Desert Marathon over 26 miles in 1995. He won a gold medal at the European championship in 1995.

Most amazingly of all, in all the miles he has covered in competition, he has only retired once – and that after 95 miles of a 100-mile event. He has done everything, and what is more, he has given everything. He is 15 and has now retired from big-time competition.

But Olly is not exactly the retiring type, naturally fit and with an appetite for the occasion. And so Trego allows him to take the occasional run-out. Everything about Sunday's event was perfect, apart from the jockey, of course, but at least he would be doing his best.

Endurance riding is a relatively new horsey sport, and the sooner it gets Olympic status the better. It is basically a race across vast areas of the surface of the Earth, but there is a very sharp twist. At prearranged points throughout the race, you must stop and present your horse to a vet.

The vet checks for pulse, rate of breathing, and soundness of limb. And if your horse fails, that's it. You're out. And right at the end, you are checked once again. You can win, and still lose. If you aren't absolutely scrupulous in your care of your horse, you can't win.

It was a singularly vile day. Rain fell without compromise, but that would help to keep the horses nice and cool, wouldn't it? So Trego took me to the stables to be introduced. Horse people say that good horses 'know' they are good, and non-horse people reject this. How can a horse understand the competitions in which he takes part? How can a horse know he has won? But horses with a long competitive history have a relish for the competitions in which they take part, which are thrilling, challenging, and filled with other horses.

And it is in movement that a horse expresses his feelings about himself and his place in the world. There was no doubt about it, Olly's bearing was lordly. He expected a certain deference from people around, he expected allowances to be made for his challenging nature; because it was not just the domestic part of him that won all these events. At bottom, it was the untamed part of him that turned all those half-chances into victories.

He was fidgeting and spinning about as we tacked him up, but as soon as I swung a leg over his back, something happened. He got serious. He knew this was business, and so he put his competition head on. Together, we walked to the start.

Feeling strong? It's one of those questions people tend to ask you just before you get on to a chance ride. 'He'll pull,' Trego said. 'You won't settle him on a loose rein, not in 15 miles.' So it was with a certain trepidation that we set out.

Horse-riding is about power. Not the power you have over the horse, but the power of the horse itself. And in every discipline, the power comes in a slightly different form. In the jumping sports, the power is, of course, in the leap. With a racehorse you have that single-stride 0–40 transition. A Grand Prix dressage horse is full of the same power, but it is expressed vertically, in the extravagant and athletic paces.

And they said 1-2-3-go, and we 1-2-3-went, and Olly and I rolled into a canter and I was at once gasping with delight, and wearing a ridiculous grin on my face; bathed in a glorious horsey glow of impossible privilege. For at once I felt that power again, and it was power that came in a new and quite different form.

It wasn't speed. It was balance, poise, and, even at the first few strides, stamina. Right from those first few strides, you felt that the horse could go on for ever. What is more, you could go on for ever with him. It would be rude not to.

The economy and balance of the pace made it easy for the rider. You didn't need to move about, just balance lightly over the withers and let him flow effortlessly beneath you. Cruising through Cirencester Great Park in the hissing rain, ducking below the withers to dodge wet whipping branches, moving and moving in an endless three-quarter time. You didn't believe that the race would ever end or that you would ever want it to.

We were leading at the first vet check, us and the King's Troop, Royal Horse Artillery, with whom we had been riding knee-to-knee. And then, alas, we mucked it up. We missed a marker and got impossibly lost, and added not much less than five miles to a five-mile leg.

To my shame, I hardly minded. Dropping the pace to Olly's easy moon-walking trot, we went on and on through the damp woods. It was a very pure joy to be with such a horse, even if our error had robbed the horse of a small triumph that he certainly deserved.

Out again on the final leg, and the horse was asked to do a little more, responding with that instinctive generosity that you find in some horses. He was a gentleman as well as a star, and he didn't pull my arms out. I did ride him on a loose rein, and it really was one of the great horsey days, for this really is one of the great horsey sports. I would like to thank Jo Trego for her incredible generosity, and Oliver's Taboo for his.

The Times
3 July 1999

35

Just Like Clint

'Mighty fine horse you have there, stranger.' I have always had a soft spot for Westerns: a pleasant nostalgia for that time that surely never quite was – but whatever it was, it was a time of horses. And I always liked those strange and haunting books of Cormac McCarthy, half in love with the dream, half obsessed with the realities of a cruel and changing world. The first book of the Border Trilogy is called – what else? – *All the Pretty Horses.*

I had been approached to try Western riding, and I was a little edgy: I didn't want to mess about, wearing dress-up clothes and riding plodders. They assured me it was nothing like that. 'But is it serious?' I asked. I still had my doubts when I arrived at the Western-style saloon. The doubts lasted precisely five seconds once I had sat on my first horse that day. No: not even that long.

I am living in a dream. It is not precisely my dream, but it is a dream all right, and I share enough of it to revel in it; more than enough to wake up a little reluctantly.

'Lope,' Chris David told me, and a nice black and white mare – an American paint that looked as if Clint had just got off it – rolled into that all-day canter that these horses are so good at. David spat a jet of tobacco juice at the sand and told me: 'Stop.'

And I adjusted body position, sat deep and called a cheery 'Ho!' and we stopped in a stride, stopped on a dime, and there was me laughing incredulously. Because the horse wore no bridle: no bit, no reins, no brakes of any kind. That is the sort of thing that Western riding is all about.

I was at Drumcoura City in the wild west of Ireland, or to be more accurate, the wild Midlands: 1,500 acres of green, green grass, 120 horses, log cabins and a saloon with little doors that go bit-bat. At the bar, the dreamer himself: an Austrian named Michael Hehle. He liked cowboy films as a boy. He taught German literature, but his real love was cowboy books. There is a German writer called Karl May who wrote 75 of them, and he wrote the words to Hehle's dream.

Hehle turned to dealing in property, but his heart was not in the Tuscan villas that he sold but out on the prairie, running cattle, sleeping under the stars in the wide open spaces. And he made enough money to set up this tourist adventure in Ireland: Ireland because the soft weather (local speak for a lot of rain) makes the grass grow for the horses.

Most people would have been content with the saloon and the tourists who can go on treks and move cattle and have good touristy fun. But Hehle's dream was too vivid for compromise.

He wanted good horses, serious horses, he wanted to lead the serious life of Western riding, not just the dressing up. And Western riding is serious all right. True, a million cowboy films have told us that it is all about yeeha-ing and heading them off at the pass, but the fact is that serious horse people are serious horse people the world over, whether they wear white jods and pearl earrings or blue jeans and a cowboy hat.

Western riding was a demonstration sport at the World Equestrian Games in Rome last year, and it will be a demonstration sport at the Olympic Games in Sydney.

The discipline for Sydney is reining, or Western dressage. It would be nice to think of Olympic bronco-busting or cow-roping, but for the meantime, it is the reining that is the brand leader. And it is as flamboyant as you could wish: no longer a parochial discipline but a global sport.

Every discipline in the horsey world tends to look at other disciplines as 'cruel'. The notion of the long-suffering cowboy horse goes pretty deep: yanked this way and that, booted about with absurd spurs, sore-mouthed, bullied and sulky.

But as my bridleless adventure shows, the exact opposite is the truth. You ride with your reins in a loop like the long stroke of the letter D, and you don't do much with your legs at all: certainly no kicking. Body position is at the heart of it. And it is wonderfully precise.

And I watched David – head trainer at Drumcours City – show me how it should be done. It is always pleasing to watch a master at work in any discipline. The horse spinning like a top, David at the centre, the still point of the turning wheel. Then the crash-halt, the transition from gallop to halt at a stride, dust everywhere and the horse back on his hocks, sitting like a dog. The reins still loose, the rider in balance.

David also showed me the beautiful discipline of cutting: you take a calf from the herd, and stop it returning to its pals. The horse, ears flat to its head, confronts the calf, the calf leaping and twisting in its urgent need to return to the herd, the horse mirroring every leap in a glorious eight-legged pas de deux, the rider imperturbable, in balance, allowing the horse to do the job.

European riding styles come from the military, and the notion that there is – must be – a right and wrong way to do everything. The Western style developed for moving cattle, and no one cares about right or wrong so long as it works.

'Slouch!' David told me. 'Look around!' But years of dressage training go very deep. But also, years of dressage training allowed me to know when a horse has been beautifully schooled. One touch on the reins and horse walks backwards, free and active. Drop your hand – only one hand on the reins, must leave one free for rolling cigarettes – and you halt. Think forwards, you move forwards, maybe a touch of the leg. Turn on the spot on that 'pivot foot' and go back in the opposite direction. These horses are touch sensitive, schooled to perfection, a joy to ride, and this is a beautiful equestrian sport without a shadow of a doubt.

But to Western riding there is more than the schooling, even more than all the pretty horses. There is a dream. A landscape of the mind. A lost notion of freedom.

David talking in a saloon afterwards about his upbringing in Arizona, his wandering cowboy life, cattle-driving, plummeting down mountains and scrambling up cliff faces to rope the cows, of his preferred rodeo discipline of team-roping, with a header, who ropes the animal's head, and a heeler, who ropes the back end.

And tales of his time with bucking horses – horses are bred specially for the task of bucking. And always back to young horses: David has a special talent for young horses.

In the round pen with David, watching him with a young filly he has ridden just three times before. 'All right, you perty I'il thing'.

And mounting up: 'I have a superstition. Always take a chew before I get on a young horse. Might be my last.'

And the filly, a touch bewildered but touchingly eager to please, walked, trotted and loped and loped to halt in a stride, all in response to the lean and angular man with the quiet manners.

'You're my girl.' Spit. 'Ain't you?'

David has done everything and worked everywhere, worked with many of the masters of Western horsemanship. And he has worked out his own method, and it is quiet and gentle and respectful and reflects a lifetime of thought and action. And he's but 21.

Riding horses is a great skill, but it is making horses that is the greater gift. 'I like just to sit in the stable for a while. Do it whenever I can.'

There is a strangeness, an other-worldliness about David: heart and mind given over to all the pretty horses. Riding horses with him was a taste of what is for ever wild, reaching out to touch what is for ever untameable.

But all the horse sports are like that. There is a touch of wildness in every horse in every discipline. Every horse brings a touch of wide open spaces to every rider. A person who has a horse has the wilderness always with him. That is the dream that all of us share.

The Times
7 August 1999

36

Wisdom and Folly

Nineteen ninety-nine was a terrible year for eventing: as I have already said, five riders were killed in falls. I wrote this piece before Burghley, attempting to say something uplifting and cheerful about the sport and the three deaths that had taken place already that year, without diminishing the dangers or the impact of these terrible things. To my and everybody else's horror, another rider was killed at this event. But I hope these words are still relevant: why we remain in thrall to the terrible beauties of the risk sports, and to the horse.

Here is this weekend's debating point. If Mephistopheles were to offer you the chance to excel at any sport of your choice, would you accept? And if so, which sport would you choose? I would certainly accept the deal, and would count it a bargain. I would choose to become a top three-day eventer, and I would cheat the Devil. My dear, they would say, he has a flying change to die for, show-jumps with micrometre precision and, over country, he seems to give a horse wings.

I would cheat the Devil because three-day eventers do not lose their souls. Neither success nor adversity spoils them – an alarming generalisation, I know. But they really do combine the best of the present and the long-gone worlds.

They have the grace and charm and modesty of bearing of an amateur; and they have the focus and method of the most exacting modern-day professional. They are good-tempered, equable, friendly, amusing and delightful; the cheeriest, best-balanced – neat double entendre – and altogether the nicest bunch you can find in any professional sporting arena.

But, alas, a pall of gloom now obscures this, the most likeable of sports. Burghley starts on Thursday, one of the most important events of the year, and the mood of depression reigns. By extension, the same gloomy mood prevails over vast areas of the horsey world. The non-horsey world has caught on: the newspapers have been filled with depressing pieces about how dreadful the whole business of horses and horse-riding really is.

I intend to dispel this pall of gloom and celebrate the horse world and everything in it. And I do so with depression in my heart. For last weekend, three-day eventing suffered its third death this season. It has been a year of horrors. There was Peta Beckett, who was as brilliant as she was gorgeous. There was Robert Slade, a dashing young Australian tipped for great things. And now Polly Phillipps, who was killed in a fall last weekend. Three-day eventing is in a state of shock. For these were three really excellent riders: experienced, knowledgeable people of flair and courage and desire to win.

There has been a great tendency to take this as an indication that death and serious injury stalk abroad the length and breadth of the horse world. Partly this is a compliment to eventers, for they, perhaps more than any other elite competitors in any other sport, seem to be just like the rest of us. There is no side to them, no swank and swagger, no big money.

They do the same things as the rest of us. And this is utterly misleading. You might just as well take the death of Ayrton Senna as indication that the entire world of the motor car is packed to the brim with lethal follies. For these three-day eventers are as much like the rest of us riders as Formula One drivers are to the parent doing the school run or the rep on the next call. They just don't seem like it.

The British Horse Trials Association has a working party on safety. I spoke to Captain Mark Phillips, one of its number, who was there when Phillipps's accident happened, and sounded still in shock. 'I wish I knew the answer,' he said. 'The fences are better designed than ever before, and are constantly improving. The safety equipment of body protectors and helmets is also better than ever before. And still accidents happen. Because, at the end of the day, it is a dangerous sport.'

This is not complacent, merely the truth. Polly Phillipps's tragic tumble took place when she rode at a fairly straightforward fence. She asked for a big stride, a big jump, and the horse did his best to oblige – but caught the top rail and flipped, and landed on top of her.

This is the sort of accident we see often in National Hunt racing but the jockeys ride with shorter stirrups and generally go faster. When a horse flips, they tend to get catapulted from the saddle. The eventer, who needs much closer control and so rides long, tends to be trapped in the saddle. Most top event riders have had a horse come down on top of them. Captain Phillips remembers two such occasions, but each time he walked away. 'I was lucky,' he said.

Mark Todd, the double Olympic champion and the sport's elder statesman as chairman of the Professional Event Riders' Association, is concerned that the new system of marking places too much emphasis on speed. 'I think there is a danger that it encourages riders to go dangerously fast,' he said.

He, too, has had his walk-away moments of not-quite horror; most notably when his horse, Just An Ace, flipped beneath him, a similar accident to Phillipps's. He plans to retire next year after more than 20 years at the top. 'I don't want to keep pushing my luck,' he said.

The problem is that this terrible trio of deaths has prompted the rest of the world to misunderstand the level of danger in the horse sports. The most notorious error is the claim that riding horses is more dangerous than riding motorbikes. This is a simple twisting of the stats. One group of figures demonstrates that, over a certain period in Australia, three-day eventing had more fatalities than motorcycle racing. Somewhat different.

In fact, figures published in the journal *Sports Exercise Injury* demonstrate clearly that by far the most fatalities in recreational pursuits come from swimming: 191 deaths between 1983 and 1992, followed by boating and sailing with 69, motor sports 65 and then horse-riding, 62. Of these, most occurred in the hunting field. There were 50 deaths from fishing.

There are also figures for injuries per 100,000 participants. Here rugby is top of the pops with 440. Football has 200, cricket, hockey and skiing all 130, netball 82, athletics 69, motor sports 58, and then, at last, after basketball and squash, comes horse-riding – on 26.

This is not to say it's safe. Let us just try and be rational and sensible and accurate about how dangerous it actually is. The true danger lies in the possibility, not of bumps and bangs, but of serious head injury. Recent dramatic improvements in headgear – compulsory in most competitions – are another step towards safer riding. The problem is that your head tends to be about ten feet from the ground, which is not a sensible place from which to start. But then horse riding is not sensible. No one is saying it is.

But nor is it criminally and stupidly dangerous. These terrible accidents certainly give one powerful pause for thought, but these were not lives lost in reckless and stupid folly. No, they were lives lost in pursuit of beauty and glory and truth. They were not lives wasted. Horses are not a safe option. But horses are not just about danger, not just about being an adrenaline junkie.

Horses give you something rather more than thrills. They give you the wild world, and that is something that we have mostly lost. They give you beauty and glory and truth. A lot of people are prepared to accept the odd risk in pursuit of such things.

The Times
28 August 1999

37

How to Be a Prodigy

The next two stories are all about the time I turned into a reporter from *Hello!* magazine. I had been pursuing both these horsey people from highly celeb backgrounds for some time: and naturally, they both happened at once. It made for a somewhat hectic week, but one highly rewarding to anybody with a liking for horses and a thick streak of curiosity.

I wouldn't have been interested in celebs who merely play at the horsey life. But in each case, this was an attempt to reach the summit of the horsey world. A famous name and a famously deep purse are not small advantages here: but, ultimately, it all comes down to horsemanship. With horses, all the money in the world can only make sure that whatever you do is spectacular – whether it is success, or failure.

There are three things you need if you are to reach the heights in sport. The first is talent, obviously. The second is the talent for having talent, that is to say, the ability to make the best of yourself in competition, rather than on the practice ground. But if a young person is to make the transition from talented child to high-achieving adult, there is a third essential: support.

Some years ago, David Hemery, the Olympic gold-medal-winning athlete, completed a book, *The Pursuit of Sporting Excellence*. His study of high achievers included in the conclusion: 'Almost universally, their upbringing was stable, secure, happy and predictable. They were well nurtured.'

It is a very hard thing to have a highly talented child. It is hard for the parents to hit the balance between support and pushiness, between wise discipline and being a Parent from Hell. And perhaps the task is made harder in a family conspicuously successful.

Charlotte Edmonds is the daughter of Noel, the television person. She is now 16 and is already competing at the highest level in dressage, the most beautiful sport of them all. Her improvement has been both rapid and sustained.

She competes at Grand Prix level, at which horses cease to walk, trot and canter and start to dance. She is national champion at two levels – the sport has a complicated structure that I won't burden you with – and she has been representing Great Britain at different levels since 1995. She was taking part in the national championships at Stoneleigh yesterday, where she placed fourth in the Prix St George on Torque of the Devil.

Dressage is a boom sport in this country and British dressage has gone from laughing-stock to knocking on the door of achievement. It is possible – though one should never say these things too loudly where tender young talent is concerned – that Edmonds will be the rider to make the breakthrough.

Who is to say? But Locarno or Arnie, a horse of dynamic muscular scope, might be the horse that takes her to the Olympic Games of 2004. That is her target, anyway.

When very young, she wanted to move up a gear from a beloved hairy pony called Pipsqueak. All right, said parents. How do you propose to get the money? She earned it by looking after the chickens and selling eggs to the family, eventually raising the cash to buy a pony that received the appropriate name of Fortune.

Fast forward to a few weeks ago, when the British junior dressage team drove out to Austria for the European championships, a convoy of vehicles. One driven by Edmonds's father, doing his job of being the normal dad of an abnormally talented child, delighted, a trifle bewildered, prepared to cheer in success and give comfort in failure.

On to a merry family lunch a day or so after the event: a family of four girls. Charlotte's mother, Helen, was the horsey one, of course – the father being a motor sports man – and horsiness does pass along the genes. The drive for success can perhaps be put down to her father's example.

And Edmonds père talking about his job in the team, of videoing the tests in the arena, which are a nice souvenir and an essential training aid to those who seek improvement. Someone was watching him: 'You're shooting this through more salt water than Jacques Cousteau ever had to deal with.' Edmonds finished as top Briton, seventh overall, with her marks more than 70 per cent, which is like a Test-match batting average of 40-plus, the boundary line between good and excellent.

You can tell an awful lot about a rider in about two seconds and the first time I saw Edmonds fille get on a horse, I almost gasped.

She is tall, of course, and rides with the classic dressage rider's long straight leg, longer than you'd believe possible. But she did more than look the part. There was an easy certainty, a fluency about her that made me think at once: by George, she's got it.

We have probably all felt this thing at some time and sometimes we are wrong and sometimes we are right. The apprentice Frankie Dettori in the finish, the first touch at speed of Michael Owen, the first boundary scored by the young David Gower. And I felt it then.

Edmonds doesn't buy her horses with eggs these days, but the horse that carries the Olympic dream and the Olympic dreamer did not come to her as a 'made' horse. He came with extravagant paces and extravagant potential; everything else is her own work. Done with a quiet certainty of purpose and a clear passion.

The Germans have always been top dogs in dressage and have scoffed at British attempts to follow them. There is a good deal less scoffing these days. Edmonds trains with a German, Klaus Rath, and it was when she was first working with him as a 13-year-old that the parents got the dreaded telephone call home: 'I'm in love.' 'And I called them three times a day, and asked them, have I told you I'm in love? And they said yes, as a matter of fact you have, and then I would call them again . . .' The recipient of this passion was, of course, Locarno or Arnie.

He is a horse to challenge, a horse of such power and scope that a rider must dig deep into herself to do right by him. Nothing is worse than riding a horse that is beyond you, something you will never grasp. You feel that you have betrayed the horse.

You need courage to take on such a horse, and self-belief. And ability, of course. Dressage is about power and flamboyance and precision. Arnie has two and a half out of three, and the third, precision, is coming with wise work, fine riding and percipient coaching.

There are naturally a few photographs about, of Edmonds in

competition. And there is one of her, sitting tall and deep and her eyes bulging like organ stops. 'Were you up for competition, by any chance?' I asked.

'I'm always like that in competition. I'm very quiet before, I like to be with the horse, just by myself. And when I get in the arena – well, once recently a huge bell started tolling in the middle of my test, and they asked me if it put me off. I didn't even hear it.' That relish for competition, that real delight in the turmoil, that ability to find in stress the finest possible performance, is what sport is all about, the horse sports as much as any, but there is a bonus with horses. With horses, you can find peace and tranquillity as well.

After lunch I swung a leg over a horse myself and Edmonds fille rode out with me. Teenagers on good terms with themselves make inspiring company. We talked horse and life and schooling – she takes her A levels this school year – and plans and dreams.

And, across the divine Devonian countryside, sheep scattering from our path, we swung back again and again to family. 'They've given me everything, they are everything.' And by everything, she did not mean money. The country estate and the pretty horses is a fine dream, but it has no point and no reality without stability. The money to buy it came from the most fleeting thing ever invented – television programmes – but the house itself is built on a rock.

The Times
18 September 1999

38

On Watership Down

It is hard to see the point of vast quantities of money. A fair bit more than your own, now that is easy to understand. But ridiculous quantities of money seem to bring as much worry as pleasure.

But with this visit to Watership Down Stud, you could see the point all right. Not the comfort and the luxury, but the challenge. And I could also see, later, over lunch, how much the rhythms of the horsey life meant to the composer himself. Horses are not just for the horsey: there is a sense in which horses fulfil a need in all of us.

For most of us, life is about making the best of what we have. It is also, for that matter, what all training of horses is about, in any discipline. A great racehorse trainer can bring the best from a selling plater and a Derby contender with equal élan; a top dressage rider will get a tune from a Grand Prix horse and my own.

To very, very few comes the chance of not making the best of what you've got – but simply making the best. A concentration entirely upon excellence: on the elite of the elite. That, so far as racehorses go, is the game-plan of Sheikh Mohammed and his Godolphin operation.

And in the breeding of racehorses, that is emphatically the game-plan of a former event rider, born Madeleine Gurdon. She is now known in circles beyond eventing, and by her married name of Madeleine Lloyd-Webber.

Last year, a yearling from her Watership Down Stud went for £2.2 million at the Houghton Sales, the biggest price paid for a British-bred yearling. It was a sign that this operation had arrived. The horse was named, modestly, Shakespeare – had his eponym been living now, would he have collaborated with her husband? – and has won his only start. Next year, his progress will be watched with more than normal interest by the people who live beneath the staggering green cliff of Watership Down.

Oh yes, there are more than rabbits breeding here these days.

And the Houghton Sales approach again – they take place from 28 to 30 September at Newmarket. The horses all look lovely to me, as they parade before us, in practice for their few heart-stopping moments in the sale ring, where an athletic walk and a steady temperament must be added to the fine figure and the magical names on the pedigree.

But to the sellers at this anxious time, nothing but the flaws – invisible to me – are evident. Madeleine Lloyd-Webber, Simon Marsh, the general manager, Terry Doherty, stud manager, were all watching with tense and worried faces. The horses walked around us, the kind September sun making each coat shine and each muscle gleam.

I knew an osteopath who once prescribed, as treatment, walking about in the garden in bare feet. You need to be grounded, he said. You need to be in touch with the earth. Horse people never need to walk about in the garden in bare feet.

It is one of the ways in which horses and horse people do a general service. Their various healthy insanities have a grounding effect on all those who live within their orbit. I thought about that at the lunch table: Andrew Lloyd-Webber talking about trees and churches and an Indian who was the best pop composer since the Beatles.

He has owned this stunning and eccentric place a fair while, of course; but I suspect that horses have given the place its purpose and meaning. The country means more when you are with country people; and especially, when you are around horses.

Madeleine comes from an anciently horsey family in Suffolk. Her sister, Mel, is an equine physiotherapist and a miraculous horsewoman: I watched her working the fine National Hunt horse Suny Bay until she had him moving like a dressage horse, getting him properly balanced the better to perceive the physical problem.

Madeleine rode at the top level of eventing, around Badminton and Burghley. Now she operates the stud and its policy of excellence.

Sell the colts, race the fillies, and then breed from them. Seek excellent mares and put them to excellent stallions: and if that was as simple as it sounds there'd be several thousand millionaires in the horsey world.

And so to this pre-lunch march-past of the yearlings. This was partly rehearsal for the sales: every sensible test of nerve is good preparation. Also, the valuing man was there to make an independent valuation of stock, which is essential for insurance. It is a known ritual.

And out they come in gleaming succession. 'Lovely athletic walker.' 'Overtracks a good 18 inches.' 'Look at that genuine head.' A genuine head means that the way the horse holds his head, and the general look of it, inspires confidence: a horse with a certain amount of decency.

These magical phrases are interspersed with magical names: Nureyev, Sadler's Wells, Nashwan . . . A top working stallion, more than any other living thing on the planet, becomes a legend: bearer of a name almost more potent than the beast himself.

The animals themselves are seldom seen; we have only distant memories of their blistering victories of long ago, and the occasional still photograph of the beast in his full-grown glory, the uncompromising expression and the huge stallion's crest along the top of the neck. These are the animals whose brief and dramatic tryst with the mare produce other animals of endless promise.

They are walked for two hours a day to build up this muscle that ripples so eye-catchingly beneath the sun-shining coats. They are fed and exercised precisely in order to produce the shape that pleases the buyers. The horses must not only look good: they must also look the part.

An eccentric colour or peculiar markings may not make the horse any slower, but it will certainly cut down the number of possible buyers. And we all know what cutting down the possible buyers does to the price. The yearlings were put back in their boxes, and away from the fraught business of the contemplation of the sales – the annual testing point of the dream so far – and the atmosphere changes abruptly to one of peace. Vast fields encircled by the double ring of post-and-rail stud fencing, the quantities of good grass.

Grass is the single most important thing in the breeding of horses. On these wide and lush expanses, the mares are grazing for two, with this year's foal at their side. It is a timeless sight: but it is all Madeleine's doing.

There were no horses here before her time: it is as if the land itself had been waiting for her. She awoke the place and gave it its purpose, and now it looks as if it has been a place for the breeding of horses since time and horses began.

I have gazed down at the place from the top of Watership Down, riding, thanks to kind invitation, the hack of Ian Balding, who trains just down the road. From this dizzying height, the stud looks what it is: a refuge from the world's madness; a hotbed of that specialised insanity of horses and racing and breeding.

Over lunch in the garden – there is a church in the garden, incidentally – it is impossible not to be struck by the energetic and leapfrogging mind of the chap that writes the music. His is a stimulating rather than a calming presence, talking now about the singer in a band of Brit-born Pakistanis.

But there is also cross-table conversation about the horses; the relentless and demanding rhythms of the horsey year are a matter of daily business, daily worry, daily pleasure. Horses are at once a matter of cosy domestic life and the wildest of impossible dreams. We are all the madder for having horses in our lives, even vicariously; and all the saner.

The Times
25 September 1999

39

Riding the Dressage Camels

The dressage camels were the runaway hit of Olympia in 1999. I was asked to write a piece about them for the news pages. Could I possibly get to meet the camels? Meet them? I wanted a chance of riding them. And so I had a beautiful morning in the company of the dancing camels.

In every field of human endeavour, you find people who want to take it all just that little bit further. Climbing Everest is too simple a task: this sort has to find a hard way and then go up it. Pinpoint marksmanship is too limited a game: followers of the extreme way shoot ancient muzzle loaders with black powder and still sometimes hit the target.

But if you seek mad endeavours, the easiest place to find them is among the people who dwell in the animal world. After all, they start closer to barking than most.

And so I sought a mad endeavour. I went to the Olympia International Show-Jumping Championships in order to ride a dressage camel. For it happens that a pair of dressage camels have taken the show by storm in a glorious combination of brilliance and absurdity.

Dressage is – at least under normal circumstances – the acme of horsemanship, the pinnacle of equine athleticism. It begins as gymnastics, passes through dance, and ends up as the kind of weightless, floating joy we touch sometimes in our dreams. It is the ultimate expression of the union of horse and human: a test, if you like, of single-mindedness, perhaps centaur-mindedness. At its highest Himalayan peak, dressage is beyond such base, Earth-bound concepts as beauty.

But camels? Great horse dressage dampens my eyes with its perfection (animal people tend to emotional lability); great camel dressage dampened my eyes for other reasons. But it was not a derisive kind of laughter: it was the laughter of delight. Human and camel moving as one. It was nothing less than a triumph of – not horsemanship. Camelmanship? Animalmanship? Never mind. The operative word is triumph.

The story of the dressage camel begins with Frank Bock, a German zookeeper. He worked in Stuttgart Zoo for 15 years as their camel man. He happened to get allocated the camels, chance being the shaping force in most people's lives. He struck up a bond with camels, just as more obvious folk strike up a bond with horses. 'They are such lovely animals,' he said.

They lack a reputation for loveliness, although that is only a reflection of our limitations. But they are not utterly safe animals. They lack the demented flight responses of horses, but camels, the stallions in particular, can be very aggressive. A keeper in Hanover Zoo was killed by his camel.

Herr Bock was intrigued by the trainability of camels; after all, camels have been domesticated for centuries, and the Prophet himself was a camel driver.

The zoo gave no encouragement, and failed to satisfy his hunger to explore the limits of the camel psyche. So he left, acquired two camels of his own, Timbu and Rani, and set about their training. After trial and error, he made a bit-less bridle that they were happy in. The dressage camels were off and waddling.

It was not easy. 'They understand what you want much faster than horses,' Herr Bock's partner, Isolde Frenzel, said. 'But it takes much longer to make them do it.' In fact, if they don't fancy being schooled for one reason or another, they will just lie down. And stay down. So there.

Kipling's marching song of the baggage camels goes: 'Can't! Don't! Shan't! Won't! / Pass it along the line! / Somebody's pack has slid from his back / Wish it were only mine!'

And Timbu, Fräulein Frenzel said, was in a bad mood. He'd had enough of going in and out of his box to please daytime television presenters who make 'jokes' about getting the hump. So I introduced myself with care. Camels spit – it's not a legend – as a mark of aggression, and Timbu has spat a fair few cuds in his time. But he was good enough to let me off that ordeal. I sat between his humps – he was sitting down – and, in the manner of a small earthquake, he stood.

So I took up the reins. That is to say I reached out to touch him.

And to my delight, he responded. He answered the very lightest of touches on the reins, moved from the pressure of the leg. 'Ride him like a horse,' Fräulein Frenzel said, and I did, for all that the for'ard hump got in the way of classical equitation.

So, incidentally, does the fact that camels move the legs of each side as a pair, a disconcerting gait; but it was lithe, athletic and pleasant to sit to. So was the camel's shambling trot, for that matter.

I got a response from him, I really did. He moved backwards when I asked, forward again when I contradicted myself, moved sideways away from my leg.

The lag in response time was odd at first, but easy enough to get used to, like steering a boat. Herr Bock was right. A lovely animal.

He and Fräulein Frenzel take their holidays with Rani and Timbu, hitching a wagon to the camels, taking a horse or two, a few friends, and visiting the wilder places. Once a cyclist fell off at their appearance. Sometimes people pass by without turning a head.

Herr Bock is a camel trainer and house-husband, Fräulein Frenzel a schoolteacher.

They give camel dressage exhibitions for a reason caught for ever between madness and love. It's taken only nine years. So far.

And oh, those flying changes. The crowd, splendidly knowledgeable, roared and squealed with delight at each appearance of this repeated miracle. A flying change – change of leading leg in canter, a dance step, a magical skip – is a pretty advanced move for a horse.

But a camel? Well – why shouldn't a camel be beautiful and athletic? Why should a camel not fulfil his potential? Why should a camel not dance?

'I think in a year,' Herr Bock said, 'he will be doing a flying change every third stride.' Very few people can get a horse to do that. I changed camels and rode Rani back to their stabling.

Dismounting, I stroked a soft grey muzzle. Briefly she touched a soft cheek to my own.

The Times
18 December 1999

40

Starting Afresh

A dog is not just for Christmas; a horse is not just for racing. Racing is a game about evolution, survival of the fittest: only the best go on to breed and become ancestors. In real life, evolution has a desperately high wastage rate; that's how it works.

But when you are playing a game about evolution, you have responsibility for the losers. At least, you should do. Welfare of the horse has an increasingly high priority in every aspect of the horsey life: and so I made a journey to visit the Thoroughbred Rehabilitation Centre.

Every year, 5,000 horses leave racing. Where do they go? It's a short question with a long answer. The best colts go on to work as stallions, the decent fillies become broodmares, some pass on to other equestrian disciplines, some leave racing because they are too badly injured to do any kind of work, and are destroyed.

And some fall into a black hole, misfits passed from hand to hand until they meet their fate, often enough the meatman. It is a problem that, until recently, no one wanted to talk about, or think about.

Oh, plenty of racehorses have a pleasant and happy retirement, often kicking about as a companion horse in an indulgent owner's field, sometimes reschooled as a hack or a hunter or a competitor in local shows, often enough by an owner's horsey daughter.

But not all owners have fields or horsey daughters, and though decent owners want to see a horse that has done its best go on to some kind of decent life, they do not always know what to do.

Five years ago, Carrie Humble, a theatrical designer by trade and a global traveller by personal history and inclination, decided that it was time to do something. She is the sort of person who makes decisions like that and when she decides, it is time for strong men to duck. So I went to visit the Thoroughbred Rehabilitation Centre (TRC), out in darkest Lancashire, and the first rehabilitated thoroughbred I clapped eyes on was Hallo Dandy. You will recall Hallo Dandy . . . he won the Grand National in 1984.

You will see at once that it is not just the forgotten no-hopers that need help. But the TRC has now converted more than 50 thoroughbreds, rescued them from the black hole and sent them back out in horsey society to live a normal, decent and merry life.

It is a job that takes an awful lot of doing. I know this with immense precision because I once did the job myself. In Hong Kong, I took on a horse who was 11, and had spent eight years racing. He had, as we horsey people say, two basic paces: stop and piss off.

He had a particularly engaging technique, which was to meander round the school until I was lulled into a false sense of security, then spin through 90 degrees and piss off at a full gallop. He was never dull, I can tell you that, but that's thoroughbreds for you.

And we ended up looking, on our good days, like very decent show-jumpers (at local show level) and at least completing a couple of two-day events. I'd like to say it was all down to my fantastic horsemanship, so I will . . . but I really ought to add that I had some rather better than fantastic help and advice. Oh, and it took me two years.

So to get 50 of them out to a new and decent life is an achievement, for these unwanted duds are also fantastic horses. The thoroughbred is a beautiful and volatile animal that has a more vivid sense of being alive than any other domestic creature on earth.

They are bred to be no more than half-tame at best and to breed out the wildness would be to breed out the yearning for dominance, the raw speed, the adrenaline surges of fight and flight, the desire to win, to be the best.

Humble started the operation up on a very small scale. You get a lot of slightly nutty people on the fringes of the horsey world, and when you read a prospectus of some good-hearted outfit like this, you sometimes wonder whether or not the whole thing is completely baked. But then I looked on the list of patrons and found the names of Lord Oaksey and Sir Peter O'Sullevan, two of the most decent people who ever patted a horse, and both of them unflinching in their commitment to the welfare of the horse.

They have, each of them, spoken up for the horse for years, and for years have put up with being regarded as slightly soft. Now it seems that their concerns are becoming mainstream. The TRC has received a number of donations and help from some of the best-known names in racing. Now something is being done about it, there seems to be a general agreement that the problem itself can be acknowledged.

The TRC gets no funding directly from racing's various official coffers – that remains a dream and a very serious ambition. But they have recently moved premises, and now occupy a good 40 acres, with plans going ahead for an indoor school. And they now have the unbelievable luxury of a real lavatory on the premises – they've been going up-market at a quite phenomenal rate, you see.

And they are, indeed, completely baked. Serious, goal-driven people. They have a waiting list of horses to come in, and a waiting list of people who want to take on one of these lapsed dream machines. But there's an awful lot to do in the middle. And it is a matter, Humble said, of 'renegotiating the contract'.

These are words that carry a lot of resonance for a lot of horsey people these days. For this is a Montyism, a phrase stolen for the horsey world by Monty Roberts, the inventor of the technique called join-up.

This renegotiating begins with a careful explanation – an explanation to the horse itself that life is changing, that the old demands have gone and new ones will be coming to take their place.

First, a dramatic reduction of tension, an introduction to a time of ease, the introduction to the life they never knew. Grazing in a field is probably something they have never done, and almost certainly not in company. And grazing and socialising are the horse's favourite things in life.

Then comes a re-education, which is more or less a re-breaking, a fresh start. Humble and her team begin with join-up, which tells them an awful lot about the horse's level of trust for human beings. The horses that join up readily with a human are likely to be easy to reschool.

And then the reschooling begins, first working on foot, with the long reins, and then riding. Some horses adapt quickly, some adapt slowly, some go on to compete and some go on to become pleasant hacks. All that succeed go on to a merry life, sparky and scintillating company for the right kind of rider.

Finding the right home is never easy. It is a fact that thoroughbreds look fab, and any rider is always going to rather fancy himself/herself on a beautiful former racehorse. I know I looked stunning on mine. Thoroughbreds are a temptation to horsey vanities of every kind.

But remember this: a thoroughbred can stop being a racehorse, but it can never stop being a thoroughbred. It will never forget what it was bred for, and what it was originally trained for. This is not everybody's ideal ride.

But for the right owner, a thoroughbred is a kind of perfection, the perfect paradox of power and nervousness, always aware, and always quite stunningly alive.

Such beings are not to be thrown away. Nor is this enterprise a sentimental filling of the field with old crocks eking out their last days in uselessness and pain. This is simply a refusal to waste a grand animal, a second chance for beasts that are challenging, gloriously stimulating.

There is a sea change of attitude taking place in racing, and in much of the horsey world. Increasingly, the debt between human and horse is seen as a two-way thing. Racehorses coming off the track can, with the TRC, renegotiate their contracts. And through organisations like this, human beings can begin to renegotiate their contract with the horse.

Postscript: The TRC has since become one of three similar

organisations that receive funding from the British Horseracing Board and other bodies in racing.

The Times
30 October 1999